Learner Autonomy

CAMBRIDGE HANDBOOKS FOR LANGUAGE TEARCHERS

This is a series of practical guides for teachers of English and other languages. Illustrative examples are usually drawn from the field of English as a foreign or second language, but the ideas and techniques described can equally well be used in the teaching of any language.

In this series:

Drama Techniques in Language Learning – A resource book of communication activities for language teachers *by Alan Maley and Alan Duff*

Games for Language Learning
by Andrew Wright, David Betteridge and Michael Buckby

Discussions that Work – Task-centred fluency practice *by Penny Ur*

Once Upon a Time – Using stories in the language classroom
by John Morgan and Mario Rinvolucri

Teaching Listening Comprehension *by Penny Ur*

Keep Talking – Communicative fluency activities for language teaching
by Friederike Klippel

Working with Words – A guide to teaching and learning vocabulary
by Ruth Gairns and Stuart Redman

Learner English – A teacher's guide to interference and other problems
edited by Michael Swan and Bernard Smith

Testing Spoken Language – A handbook of oral testing techniques
by Nic Underhill

Literature in the Language Classroom – A resource book of ideas and activities
by Joanne Collie and Stephen Slater

Dictation – New methods, new possibilities *by Paul Davis and Mario Rinvolucri*

Grammar Practice Activities – A practical guide for teachers *by Penny Ur*

Testing for Language Teachers *by Arthur Hughes*

Pictures for Language Learning *by Andrew Wright*

Five-Minute Activities – A resource book of short activities
by Penny Ur and Andrew Wright

The Standby Book – Activities for the language classroom *edited by Seth Lindstromberg*

Lessons from Nothing – Activities for language teaching with limited time and resources
by Bruce Marsland

Beginning to Write – Writing activities for elementary and intermediate learners
by Arthur Brookes and Peter Grundy

Ways of Doing – Students explore their everyday and classroom processes
by Paul Davis, Barbara Garside and Mario Rinvolucri

Using Newspapers in the Classroom *by Paul Sanderson*

Teaching English Spelling – A practical guide *by Ruth Shemesh and Sheila Waller*

Learner Autonomy

A guide to developing learner responsibility

Ágota Scharle
Anita Szabó

CAMBRIDGE
UNIVERSITY PRESS

PUBLISHED BY THE PRESS SYNDICATE OF THE UNIVERSITY OF CAMBRIDGE
The Pitt Building, Trumpington Street, Cambridge, United Kingdom

CAMBRIDGE UNIVERSITY PRESS
The Edinburgh Building, Cambridge CB2 2RU, UK   http://www.cup.cam.ac.uk
40 West 20th Street, New York, NY 10011–4211, USA   http://www.cup.org
10 Stamford Road, Oakleigh, Melbourne 3166, Australia
Ruiz de Alarcón 13, 28014 Madrid, Spain

First published 2000

Printed in the United Kingdom at the University Press, Cambridge

Typeset in Sabon 10.5/12 pt [VN]

*A catalogue record for this book is available
from the British Library*

Library of Congress Cataloguing in Publication data applied for

ISBN 0 521 77534 5 paperback

Contents

Thanks and acknowledgements

We would like to thank Penny Ur for her editorial guidance and support and Caroline Bodóczky, Jackie Mattonen, and Judit Zerkowitz for all their suggestions and encouragement.

Initial drafts of the book were prepared with the help of a grant from the Közoktatási Modernizációs Közalapítvány, Hungary, for which we are most grateful.

The authors and publishers are grateful to the following for permission to reproduce copyright material. It has not been possible to identify the sources of all the material used and in such cases the publishers would welcome information from copyright owners.

Extracts on pp. 6, 55–56, 70–71 and 91 from *A Guide to Student-Centred Learning* by D. Brandes & P. Ginnis, Simon and Schuster 1992. Reproduced by permission of Pearson Publishing; Extracts on pp. 17 and 72 from *Roles of Teachers and Learners* by Tony Wright © Oxford University Press 1987. Reproduced by permission of Oxford University Press; Extracts on pp. 18 and 57 *Teaching how to learn: A Teacher's Guide* by Ken Willing. Reproduced by permission of the National Centre for English Language Teaching and Research (NCELTR), Australia © Macquarie University; 'Guessing hidden strengths' on p. 26 from *The Confidence Book* by Davis & Rinvolucri, Longman 1990. Reproduced by permission of the authors; 'Check your facts' on p. 69 from *Teaching English Pronunciation* by J. Kenworthy, © Longman Group UK Limited 1987. Reprinted by permission of Pearson Education Limited; Quote on p. 102 from *Byron, a Portrait* by Leslie Marchand. Reproduced by permission of John Murray (Publishers) Ltd; Quotes on p. 102 from *The Life of John Maynard Keynes*, by Roy Harrod. Copyright 1951 by R. F. Harrod. Reproduced by permission of W. W. Norton & Company Inc.

Introduction

Most language teachers have experienced the frustration of investing endless amounts of energy in their students and getting very little response. We have all had groups who never did their homework, who were reluctant to use the target language in pair or group work, who did not learn from their mistakes, who did not listen to each other, who did not use opportunities to learn outside the classroom, and so on.

Such behaviour very often stems from one common cause: the learners' over-reliance on the teacher. Even otherwise motivated learners may assume a passive role if they feel the teacher should be in charge of everything that happens in the classroom.

This book offers language teachers practical guidance on how to develop a sense of responsibility in their learners so that they will understand why and how they learn and be willing to take an active role in their learning. The task is not an easy one, as training learners for responsibility involves changing their attitudes.

This is reflected in the organisation of the book as well as in the design of the activities. We grouped activities into three sections representing the three phases of the development process. First, the learners have to become aware of the difference their contribution can make, and of the nature of language learning in general (*Raising awareness*). Second, they need some well-structured practice in their new attitudes as responsible learners (*Changing attitudes*) so that, in the third phase, they will be ready to take over some roles from the teacher and enjoy the freedom that comes with increased responsibility (*Transferring roles*).

In all three phases, the activities work on familiar targets of learner development, such as motivation, learning skills, empathy, and cooperation. The novelty of our approach lies in the systematic combination of such targets, and in its emphasis on gradual development. Rather than advocating the abolition of teacher control or radical changes in classroom management, the book focuses on the slow process of changing attitudes.

A common worry about similar learner development programmes is that they require a lot of extra time, which is already in short supply in most teaching situations. Aware of this constraint, we designed all the activities to blend into the regular curriculum, serving many purposes

1

from skills training to grammar practice. Thus the book can be used as a handy supplement to any course book. To help reduce preparation time, the Appendix provides photocopiable materials for use in the activities.

We offer the book especially to our fellow-teachers in Eastern Europe, and others working in an environment where frontal teaching dominates, or with students whose past experience is dominantly in frontal teaching. Though some of the activities may be used with children, most of them work best with teenage to adult learners, and the approach is most effective if used in longer courses, typically in formal education.

PART 1

1.1 Responsibility and autonomy

This section is a brief overview of the ideas and problems connected to training learners for responsibility. For the reader wishing to learn about these issues in more depth or detail, we included an annotated list of further reading at the end of the section.

What makes a responsible learner?

How would you describe responsible learners? Do they always do their homework and follow the teacher's instructions? Are they good team workers? Or do they volunteer to clean the blackboard? Are they diligent and obedient? They may not always be like that.

We do not think of responsible learners as role models (or teacher's pets), but as learners who *accept the idea that their own efforts are crucial to progress in learning, and behave accordingly.* So, when doing their homework or answering a question in class, they are not aspiring to please the teacher, or to get a good mark. They are simply making an effort in order to learn something.

Responsible learners do not have to be especially keen on team work, but they *are willing to cooperate with the teacher and others in the learning group for everyone's benefit.* Cooperation does not mean that they always obediently follow instructions: they may ask about the purpose of the activity first, or they may even come up with suggestions on how to improve an activity.

Finally, responsible students may not always do their homework, but whenever they fail to do it, they are aware of missing an opportunity to expand their knowledge of the foreign language. This is because they *consciously monitor their own progress, and make an effort to use available opportunities to their benefit, including classroom activities and homework.*

This last point leads us to the question of defining autonomy. We had a heated discussion about this when writing this section, trying to agree on where responsibility ends, and where autonomy starts.

What makes an autonomous learner?

In theory, we may define autonomy as the freedom and ability to manage one's own affairs, which entails the right to make decisions as well. Responsibility may also be understood as being in charge of something, but with the implication that one has to deal with the consequences of one's own actions. Autonomy and responsibility both require active involvement, and they are apparently very much interrelated.

In practice, the two concepts are more difficult to distinguish. Consider, for example, these three actions:

- interrupting the teacher's explanation to ask about a certain point in the explanation
- looking up a word at home that the teacher used in the lesson but did not 'teach'
- paying special attention when the lesson is about something that the learner is not so good at.

In all these actions, learners behave responsibly as they are consciously making an effort to contribute to their learning. They are also autonomous in the sense that they act independently of the teacher, not waiting to be told what to do.

We may conclude that, in order to foster learner autonomy, we clearly need to develop a sense of responsibility and also, encourage learners to take an active part in making decisions about their learning.

Why should you develop responsibility and autonomy?

The saying goes: you can bring the horse to water, but you cannot make him drink. In language teaching, teachers can provide all the necessary circumstances and input, but learning can only happen if learners are willing to contribute. Their passive presence will not suffice, just as the horse would remain thirsty if he stood still by the river waiting patiently for his thirst to go away. And, in order for learners to be actively involved in the learning process, they first need to realise and accept that success in learning depends as much on the student as on the teacher. That is, they share responsibility for the outcome. In other words, success in learning very much depends on learners having a responsible attitude.

Some degree of autonomy is also essential to successful language learning. No matter how much students learn through lessons, there is always plenty more they will need to learn by practice, on their own. Also, the changing needs of learners will require them to go back to learning several times in their lives: then again, they will need to be able to study on their own. The best way to prepare them for this task is to help them become more autonomous.

How far can you go?

We think of autonomy or responsibility as attitudes that students may possess to varying degrees. No student is completely without a sense of responsibility and we are not likely to meet in person the ideal student, either. Personality traits, preferred learning styles, and cultural attitudes set limits to the development of autonomy.

Individual students or the community they come from may have a strong aversion to individualism and a preference for collectivism, so they may be unwilling to take personal initiative. Some students may not be able to handle uncertainty and do everything they can to avoid it, so they may find it alarming to work without the constant supervision of the teacher, or they may detest all open-ended tasks, where there is no one correct answer. Some other students may look at the teacher as a figure of authority who is always there to tell them what to do.

How can you adapt to new teacher roles?

Developing responsible attitudes in the learner entails some deviation from traditional teacher roles as well. As students begin to take charge of their learning, the teacher needs to take on the role of facilitator or counsellor in an increasing number (and type) of classroom situations.

You may find it useful to think over your existing attitudes. One way to do this is to confront yourself with the extreme views of the traditional and the learner centred approaches. You may also consider classroom tasks, and the way you share responsibility for their accomplishment between yourself and your students. (We included a list of typical tasks in the Appendix on page 101.) Look at the table on page 6 and try to put yourself somewhere along the continuum between the two extremes.

We would encourage you to experiment with moving towards the right hand side of the continuum. Learner responsibility can really only develop if you allow more room for learner involvement.

However, the change in your roles can be or perhaps should be gradual, rather than abrupt and dramatic. The school where you teach, the community of teachers, the parents of the students and the students themselves will have expectations about what roles a teacher is supposed to perform. These expectations may be very different from the teacher roles that facilitate learner responsibility, and if this is the case, changing them will require much patience and caution.

You may find that people oppose changes for different reasons, and not necessarily because they are against your aims. They may be afraid of the uncertainties and risks involved in changes in general, or they may have had negative experiences with some other alternative teaching methods

Traditional attitudes	My attitude	Student centred attitudes
I have all the information.		The syllabus, the exam, and the information are here for us to share.
It is my job to transmit knowledge to you.		I am not the fount of all knowledge.
I am responsible for your learning.		You are responsible for your learning.
It is my job to make sure that you work.		I am here to facilitate your learning by providing resources and support.
As the adult, and the professional, I have the expertise to make the right judgements and decisions about your learning.		I trust that you want to learn and will take responsibility for your own learning.

(Adapted from Brandes and Ginnis, 1992.)

and are therefore suspicious of any such initiative. Some people may fear the loss of their authority, and some might be jealous of your increased popularity among students. Parents or teachers may also oppose the increase of learner involvement because they fear that it leads to disorder, lack of respect for adults, or less efficient teaching.

In any case, head-on collision is likely to provoke strong reactions, and then it may become very difficult to sort out the real reasons behind the conflict and soothe opponents. If you take a gradual approach, then there is ample time for everybody to get used to the change, and for you to learn about the feelings and opinions of any opponents and find ways to deal with these. Also, with a quiet start you may be able to produce some results and win supporters, before any resistance springs up.

To prevent or deal with strong negative reactions, we recommend that you:

- think about who may respond negatively to the changes you propose and why,
- try taking the viewpoint of any potential opponents and think about how you could lower their apprehension or aversion,
- accept the validity of other teaching methods, and be ready to compromise,
- share information about what you are doing or planning to do with your superiors, colleagues, parents, and (perhaps most importantly) your students,

- involve your colleagues as much as possible by sharing your problems and discussing your experiments with them, and
- be receptive to suggestions and criticism.

Support from colleagues in your school or elsewhere who are involved in a similar training programme may also help you to survive critical periods.

How can you develop responsibility and autonomy?

The activities in this book are designed to achieve two things. They help learners to realise the importance of their contribution and they develop the abilities learners will need to take charge of their own learning. Let us consider each skill and attitude that we have identified as building blocks of responsibility and autonomy.

Motivation and self-confidence: We have earlier quoted the example of the horse taken to the river to drink, and explained that unless he is willing to do his part (lower his head to reach the river and take in some water), the horse will remain thirsty. Here we may add that the project will also fail if the horse is not thirsty at all. In other words, *motivation* is a prerequisite for learning and responsibility development alike. However, for our purposes not any kind of motivation will do.

We need to encourage *intrinsic* motivation, the source of which is some inner drive or interest of the learner. Intrinsically motivated learners are more able to identify with the goals of learning and that makes them more willing to take responsibility for the outcome. In turn, a larger scope for student self-determination and autonomy generates intrinsic motivation. In other words, motivation and responsibility can mutually reinforce each other.

It is important to note that rewards and punishment (*extrinsic* motivation) can also stimulate learning, but at the same time they increase the dependence of the learner.

Apart from reinforcing motivation, *self-confidence* contributes to the development of responsibility in its own right. The learners must believe that they are capable of managing their own learning and they can rely on themselves, not only on the teacher. The effect works the other way as well: a feeling of responsibility and independence brings a sense of well-being and confidence.

Monitoring and evaluation: When we encourage students to focus on the *process* of their learning (rather than the *outcome*) we help them consciously examine their own contribution to their learning. Such an awareness of the difference that their efforts can make is an essential first step to the development of a responsible attitude.

Self-evaluation requires the learners to go even further: they have to step into the shoes of the teacher and judge their own work as objectively as they can. By doing so, they can formulate an idea of their level of proficiency: discover weak and strong points and plan the directions of progress. Setting targets for themselves, they are more likely to consider these targets their own and feel responsible for reaching them.

Learning strategies serve as tools to improve one's language competence, and learners can really only be held responsible for their competence if they are aware of these tools. So, we need to show students the variety of available strategies, help them to find out what works for them, and help them to discover how and when to use these strategies. We can bring students to the thrilling experience of exploring and expanding their own abilities.

Cooperation and group cohesion: Promoting cooperation in the classroom affects learner attitudes in several ways. It encourages the learners to rely on each other (and consequently themselves as well) and not only on the teacher. Group work also creates opportunities for feedback from peers: learners will do things to please the group rather than to please the teacher. Finally, pair and group work (as compared to whole class work) may help you to get a higher proportion of students actively involved in completing a task.

These then are the building blocks of responsible attitudes on the part of the learner. But the development process also requires a certain teacher attitude: a willingness to take learners as partners in achieving common goals, consistency in control, and a willingness to delegate tasks and decisions. Let us now consider these.

Sharing information with the learner: By sharing all the relevant information with students, teachers express respect and a willingness to regard learners as partners in working towards the common aim of learning a foreign language. This includes being very clear about both short and long term objectives. Telling students about the aim(s) of a particular activity helps them to identify with these aims and hence to feel more responsible for the outcome.

Consistent control: It is very important to clearly establish expectations towards the learner, the limits of acceptable behaviour and the consequences of failing to meet expectations. You may find that, as long as you apply rules consistently, learners are willing to play by these rules. But, make sure not to tighten your control too much, as that may stifle all learner initiative.

Delegating tasks and decisions: If learners are to take more responsibility for their learning, they need to have more influence on the learning process. This calls for a reallocation of some tasks and decisions in classroom work, so that students can get more involved for example in choosing learning materials or correcting mistakes. Students are of course not trained teachers and cannot take over *any* teacher role, but they are surely able to cope with some of the teacher's roles. It is important that the teacher should respect the ways they handle these tasks, and expect learners to deal with the consequences of their decisions. Support them but do not rescue them or, in other words, do not be afraid to let them make mistakes.

Stages in the process of developing learner responsibility

People do not normally wake up to a fine day and find that they have become responsible overnight. More likely, they go through a slow, gradual process as they are approaching adulthood. We divided this process into the following three phases:

- *Raising awareness* is the starting point. Here we present new viewpoints and new experiences to the learners and encourage them to bring the inner processes of their learning to the conscious level of their thinking. We are trying to bring them to discoveries: 'Wow, this is interesting!' or, 'So, that's the way it is!'

  Most of the activities at this stage are rather tightly structured, and controlled by the teacher. This is because we assume that learners are not yet very responsible: they need to be told what to do.
- The next step is practising the skills introduced at the previous stage in order to begin *changing attitudes*. This is a slow process requiring a lot of practice and patience, since it takes time to go from understanding to practising new roles and habits, especially when this involves breaking away from stubborn old patterns of behaviour. Learners who have little sense of responsibility in general require particular attention and patience.

  Many of the activities at this stage are repeatable, and they tend to allow more room for learner initiative.
- *Transferring roles* to the learner requires a considerable change in classroom management and so it may be the most demanding phase for the teacher.

  The activities are loosely structured, giving a considerable amount of freedom to the students in accomplishing tasks, or even, in deciding about tasks.

We see this as a smooth process where one phase develops into the next. So, even though we want the learner to be aware of the process as a whole and the actual changes within each phase, the transition from one phase to the other is not some momentous event that may be announced as an achievement.

The use of integrated and explicit training

Learner training may take the form of an optional course offered to interested students, or may be incorporated into a regular language course. A further choice is whether to develop skills and attitudes implicitly, that is, helping students to use strategies but not actually discussing these strategies with them, or explicitly, with the conscious participation of the learners.

We have chosen to integrate responsibility development into the regular curriculum for three very practical reasons. First, combining learner development with regular curricular aims may save a lot of time and money. Second, there are always some not particularly motivated students who would never volunteer to attend a learner training course. Meeting them in the regular, obligatory classes, we may 'get them on our side' even before they notice. Third, we can use the contents of the regular school curriculum as a meaningful context for strategy training.

Throughout the development process, and especially in the teaching of learning strategies, we recommend that students are taught skills and attitudes explicitly. This is because we believe that awareness and reflection are essential for the development of responsibility. Explicit training may also encourage a collaborative spirit between the teacher and the learner. Finally, in the case of learning strategies, the conscious realisation of what strategies are applied in a given activity may increase the chances of transfer to other tasks.

1.2 How to use the book

The activities

The activities are presented in three sections according to the stages of developing responsible learner attitudes: raising awareness, changing attitudes, and transferring roles. At the beginning of each subsection, we briefly explain the general aims of the activities included, the underlying rationale, and some further suggestions on how to use them. Within the sections we have grouped activities according to what aspect of responsibility they tackle. The three sections follow the recommended chronological order of applying the activities, while activities within the sections can be used in any order, as it seems appropriate.

The outline of each activity begins with a list of basic characteristics:

- *level* shows the difficulty of the activity in terms of required language proficiency (indicated if the activity is only applicable to particular levels)
- *main goals* describe the attitude or skill the activity is designed to tackle
- *language focus* indicates other curricular objectives, such as grammar practice and subskills of speaking, listening, reading, and writing
- *preparation* lists materials or devices you may need for the activity, such as handouts or tapes
- *notes* may include some other useful information on the activity

In some cases the instructions on how to carry out the activity are followed by further suggestions on possible variations. For example, these may be adaptations to a different level of linguistic ability or to a different group size.

Some activities are supplied with photocopiable sample materials, which are usually placed next to the activity, and in a few cases in the Appendix. Finally, the Index helps you find activities for particular areas of grammar, skills practice, or specific topics.

Starting out

You may already have a fairly precise understanding of your learners' attitudes towards learning if you have had time to observe their work in class. Do they ask questions? Do they respond quickly to instructions? Do they do their homework? Do they listen to you when you correct their mistakes?

Still, you may find it useful to begin by collecting some information on the existing attitudes and expectations of your learners. Especially with a class that seems unreceptive to a teaching style that would require considerable activity from the learners, you will need a lot of careful preparation. What sorts of experiences have they had with other teachers? What sorts of activities are they used to? In section 2.1.1 (pages 16–24) we have included some examples of how you may collect such information.

Finding out about your learners' expectations will help you to devise a gradual introduction of new elements into your teaching, and you may be better able to deal with your students' reactions.

You may experiment first with some activities and embark on a systematic implementation of the development programme once you have confidence in the book. It is probably best to try the new approach with new groups, where the allocation of tasks and decisions between you and the learners is yet to be established.

Planning ahead

Once you know how responsible your learners already are, you need to decide what skills and attitudes need most attention, and how much time you can allot to training your learners for responsibility. It may be useful to include some awareness exercises into your programme even with already fairly autonomous learners, as bringing the use of skills and attitudes to the conscious level can help further development. With such a group however, you may need to spend less time on the second, practice stage. There is no general rule as to which activities to pick from the third section. Your choice of what teacher roles to transfer to students will depend on your personality, your views on teaching, the learners' inclinations, and the institutional environment.

It is perhaps best if you start by doing one or two awareness exercises each week, over one or two months, depending on how many lessons per week you teach and on which areas students need more awareness raising. For example, working on learning strategies may take a bit longer than increasing self-confidence. When you move on to practice activities, you may try and do as many as you can fit into the regular syllabus. Students will probably need at least two months to feel comfortable with the new attitudes and skills they have started to develop. When you feel the time is ripe, you can start experimenting with transferring roles. Then, depending on how students respond, you may move back to have a little more practice, or continue with transferring more demanding roles.

We recommend that you involve the learners in planning the development process as much as possible. Explain your plans concerning the development process, and give them an opportunity to respond. This is of course not to say that they have to understand all the underlying methodology and theory. It may be enough to say that they will not only learn English with you, but also some skills and techniques for learning the language, and they will find out about which of these work best for them. Especially with more mature students, you may offer some options within the plan which they can choose from. This may not be easy, as decision making requires the learners to take some responsibility, and you may also find it difficult to accept and accommodate their preferences. Too high demands on the learners may frighten or alienate them. However, a careful, gradual involvement can increase their motivation and interest in the development activities.

Further reading

Benson, Phil and Voller, Peter (eds.) (1997) *Autonomy and Independence*, Longman includes articles on the cultural and philosophical aspects of autonomy, on the roles of teachers and learners, and on methods and materials fostering autonomy. See especially Esch, Edit M., *Learner training for autonomous language learning*, Voller, Peter, *Does the teacher have a role in autonomous language learning?*, and Nunan, David, *Designing and adapting materials to encourage learner autonomy*.

Brandes, Donna and Ginnis, Paul (1990) *The Student-Centred School*, Basil Blackwell Ltd explores the problems teachers working in a rigid or unreceptive school may encounter and suggests ways to deal with these. Also includes activities for teacher workshops.

Brandes, Donna and Ginnis, Paul (1992) *A Guide to Student-Centred Learning*, Simon and Schuster Education may also help you in dealing with unreceptive students or colleagues.

Carver, David and Dickinson, Leslie (1993) *Learning to be self-directed* in: Geddes, Marion and Sturtridge, Gill (eds.) (1993) *Individualisation*, Modern English Publications Ltd offers a clear explanation of what responsibility means, an overview of techniques, and some examples for activities.

Cotterall, Sarah (1995) 'Developing a course strategy for learner autonomy', *ELT Journal*, **49**, 3 discusses the need for autonomy development and reports the results of a project.

Dörnyei, Zoltán (1994) 'Motivation and motivating in the Foreign Language Classroom', *Modern Language Journal*, **78**, Autumn discusses motivation, self-confidence, learner autonomy, and cooperation in the language classroom, along with related problems and some practical advice.

Ellis, Gail and Sinclair, Barbara (1989) *Learning to Learn English*, Cambridge University Press offers step by step training for responsibility mostly focusing on learning skills and the cognitive involvement of students.

Meichenbaum, Donald and Biemiller, Andrew (1998) *Nurturing Independent Learners, Helping Students Take Charge of Their Learning*, Cambridge MA, Brookline Books provides a general theory of the development of learner autonomy in education.

O'Malley, J. Michael and Chamot, Anna Uhl (1990) *Learning Strategies in Second Language Acquisition*, Cambridge University Press reviews the literature on learning strategies.

Oxford, Rebecca (1990) *Language Learning Strategies*, Heinle and Heinle Publishers provides a careful definition of learning strategies, a comprehensive taxonomy, and suggests further contact points.

Prodromou, Luke (1992) *Mixed Ability Classes*, Macmillan offers mostly theory and some activities, and includes a chapter on learner responsibility. May be a good supplement for teacher awareness.

Reid, Joy M. (1995) *Learning Styles in the English as a Second Language Classroom*, Heinle and Heinle offers a thorough discussion of different approaches to learning styles.

Spolsky, Bernard (1989) *Conditions for Second Language Learning*, Oxford University Press provides general theory, including a section on motivation and attitudes.

Stevick, Earl W. (1976) *Success with Foreign Languages: Seven Who Achieved It and What Worked for Them*, Newbury Publishers is a very instructive study of different types of successful learners.

Tudor, Ian (1996) *Learner Centredness as Language Education*, Cambridge University Press offers a thorough, mostly theoretical discussion of the need for learner centredness, and how teachers can cope with innovations and changes in their roles.

Wenden, Anita (1991) *Learner Strategies for Learner Autonomy*, Hemel Hempstead, Prentice Hall offers ideas for teachers to prepare themselves for transferring some roles.

Wright, Tony (1987) *Roles of Teachers and Learners*, Oxford University Press includes a theoretical discussion and some activities for teacher awareness, and how to change division of roles.

PART 2

2.1 Raising awareness

The following activities are all aimed at opening the learners' eyes to new ways of thinking about their learning. Some activities invite them to consider old routines or habits at the conscious level of their thinking, e.g. how they usually memorise words. Other activities help them to discover new aspects of learning, e.g. trying out new techniques for memorising words.

The efficiency of teaching very much depends on learners' motivation, skills, and willingness or ability to cooperate and work as a community. These are also areas that we explore in this section in order to help learners realise *how* they can contribute to their learning.

The first group of activities 'Finding out about your students' outlines various techniques of collecting information about the existing attitudes and knowledge of your students. Based on the information you collect, you can decide which are the areas where awareness raising is most needed, and which are the ones where you can move straight on to the practice stage.

Activities in the second group called 'Motivation' aim to give confidence to and motivate students by emphasising skills and knowledge they already possess. We also included here two activities to help students realise and come to terms with the fact that difficulties are a natural part of learning.

Next, in 'Learning strategies' we designed some experiments to introduce learning strategies. These help students experience that such strategies can help them a lot in their learning, to think consciously about their choice of strategies, and to find out what works best for them.

'Community building' includes some activities to demonstrate the importance of listening to and cooperating with others in pair and group work, and to help students learn about views or tastes they share with others in the group.

At the end of the section, in 'Self-monitoring' you can find some examples of how to get your students to think about their learning styles, and make them aware that their group mates may have rather different preferences and use a variety of strategies.

The introductory and follow-up part of the activities are especially important. In most cases it is useful to tell your students what it is that they are going to experience, and it is worthwhile to set aside some time for a follow-up discussion (in the learners' mother tongue, if necessary) about what they discovered with the help of the activity. We usually suggest some questions to get your students to talk.

Some of the activities may surprise your students: that is all right as long as the surprise comes at least partly from the realisation you wanted to bring about. If, however, the unusual organisation or nature of the exercise attracts much more attention than the awareness component, it has missed the target. You may put to use what you have learnt about the expectations and previous experience of your students and choose activities in which their attention would not be too much occupied by the novelty of the task.

2.1.1 Finding out about your students

It is important to know what experiences your students have had and as a consequence what expectations they may have of you as a teacher. Also, information on your students' existing attitudes to learning and to the foreign language is the starting point for developing responsible attitudes. There are several ways to collect such information, and it is best if you vary these ways, otherwise the students get bored and may not take their answers seriously.

The questions in the activities below can be easily converted into another form, though in some cases the form we chose seemed to fit the given topic best. For example, you may turn the interview activity on teaching styles into a questionnaire, but you may find it difficult to include all possible variations, and thus lose some useful data.

Ready made questionnaires
answering questions on learning styles and activities

Main goal	collecting information
Language focus	reading comprehension
Preparation	handouts

You may ask students to fill in the questionnaires in the lesson, or, to save classroom time, you may assign them for homework. If you find any of them too difficult for your students to do in the foreign language, you may use a translated version, as the emphasis here is on the collection of information rather than on language practice.

1. Questionnaire to survey past experience

Please read the questions carefully and answer as many as you can.

Did your last language teacher always explain every point to you?	YES/NO/DON'T KNOW
Did you have to guess rules/meanings yourself?	YES/NO/DON'T KNOW
Did your last language teacher ever ask you to work in pairs or groups?	YES/NO/DON'T KNOW
Did your last language teacher usually stand at the front of the class when he/she was teaching?	YES/NO/DON'T KNOW
Did your last language teacher speak the foreign language most of the time in a lesson?	YES/NO/DON'T KNOW
Did you ever have to speak/write about yourself in the English lesson or as homework?	YES/NO/DON'T KNOW
Did you get an extra task or a bad mark if you did not do your homework?	YES/NO/DON'T KNOW
Did you ever have to correct/mark the work of another pupil?	YES/NO/DON'T KNOW
Did your teacher ever ask for your opinion about what to do in the lesson or how you would like to learn?	YES/NO/DON'T KNOW
Did you often use other materials in the lesson (or only the textbook)?	YES/NO/DON'T KNOW

What did you especially like or dislike about the way you were taught?

. . . .

. . . .

(Based on Wright, 1987 p. 134.) © Cambridge University Press 2000

Learning styles include perception preferences, which can be grouped into three categories: auditory (hearing), visual (seeing), and kinaesthetic (sensing bodily movement). The last one is sometimes divided into haptic (touching) and emotive (feeling, which is often connected to body reactions). You may also consider other dimensions in learning styles, like someone's attitude to other people (extraversion or introversion) and preferred routines of logic (deductive or inductive). The questionnaire overleaf is based on a mixture of these dimensions.

2. Questionnaire on learning styles

Please read the sentences carefully, and tick the ones that apply to you.

a)

In class, I like to learn by games.

In class, I like to learn by pictures, films, video.

I like to learn the foreign language by talking in pairs.

I like to go out with the class and practise the foreign language.

At home, I like to learn by using cassettes.

In class, I like to listen and use cassettes.

b)

I like to study grammar.

At home, I like to learn by studying foreign language books.

I like to study the foreign language by myself (alone).

I like the teacher to let me find my mistakes.

I like the teacher to give us problems to work on.

At home, I like to learn by reading newspapers.

c)

I like to learn by watching, listening to foreign language speakers.

I like to learn by talking to friends in the foreign language.

At home, I like to learn by watching TV in the foreign language.

I like to learn by using the foreign language in shops, on the phone, . . .

I like to learn the foreign language words by hearing them.

In class, I like to learn by conversations.

d)

I like the teacher to explain everything to us.

I want to write everything in my notebook.

I like to have my own textbook.

In the foreign language class, I like to learn by reading.

I like to study grammar.

I like to learn new words by seeing them.

(Adapted from Willing, 1989.)   © Cambridge University Press 2000

Key:
Each group of sentences corresponds to a learning style, as follows:
a) Concrete b) Analytical c) Communicative d) Authority oriented. Most students are characterised by a mixture of two or three styles, with a dominant one among them.

3. Questionnaire on responsible attitudes

This questionnaire has two parts: the first one asking about the learner and the second one about the group in general. Some students may tend to overrate themselves, trying to please the teacher: take this into account when you evaluate the first part. Use the second part as a description of the general mood or norms of behaviour in the classroom. Work out the result by adding up the numbers for questions 2, 3, and 5, and deducting the numbers for 1, 4, and 6. The maximum score is 15, indicating a very responsible student, and the minimum score is –15, indicating an alarmingly irresponsible one.

Explain to students that you would like to learn about their attitudes towards learning the foreign language, and you would like them to fill in a questionnaire as honestly as they can. Make it clear that it will not affect their marks in any way. Give each of them a copy of the questionnaire. If necessary, explain the first sentence. (They should first decide how they rate their own knowledge – good or bad – and then decide how much that can be explained by having had good or bad teachers.) The second part may also need some explaining: students shouldn't worry about describing individual classmates, but the general atmosphere in the class.

---

3. Questionnaire on responsible attitudes

Read the sentences carefully. If you completely agree, circle 6. If you do not agree at all, circle 1.

As for me . . .

the reason why I am good (bad) at the foreign language, is because I have had good (bad) teachers.	1 2 3 4 5 6
I know what I should practise more in the foreign language.	1 2 3 4 5 6
I pay more attention to the lesson if we are practising something I am not so good at.	1 2 3 4 5 6
I want only to survive the language lesson.	1 2 3 4 5 6
sometimes I learn/read things that the teacher did not give as a task.	1 2 3 4 5 6

I do as little as possible for my homework.   1 2 3 4 5 6

it is important for *me* to learn the foreign language (not only   1 2 3 4 5 6
for my parents' sake or for the marks).

As for most of the others in the class . . .

the reason why they are good (bad) at the foreign language, is   1 2 3 4 5 6
because they have had good (bad) teachers.

they know what they should practise more in the foreign lan-   1 2 3 4 5 6
guage.

they pay more attention to the lesson if we are practising   1 2 3 4 5 6
something they are not so good at.

they want only to survive the language lesson.   1 2 3 4 5 6

sometimes they learn/read things that the teacher did not give   1 2 3 4 5 6
as a task.

they do as little as possible for their homework.   1 2 3 4 5 6

it is important for them to learn the foreign language (not only   1 2 3 4 5 6
for their parents' sake or for the marks).

4. Questionnaire on attitudes towards learning the foreign language

Please read the sentences carefully and finish them with the adverb that best
applies to you.

I enjoy learning the foreign language	very much / quite a lot / not much / not at all
In my language learning this year I expect to do	very well / quite well / not badly / poorly
We waste a lot of time in the foreign language class	very often / sometimes / never
In five years' time my command of the foreign language will be	much better / a little better / the same / worse
I like the people in my language class	very much / quite a lot / not much / not at all
I would like to visit / have friends from a country where the foreign language is spoken	very much / quite a lot / not much / not at all
I would like to live in a country where the foreign language is spoken	very much / quite a lot / not much / not at all

Is there anything else you find important about your feelings towards the
target language, or the people who speak the target language?

. . . .

5. Strengths and weaknesses analysis

This questionnaire can give you important information on your students' perception of their command of the foreign language, and it can also be a first step to get your students to think about their learning.

---

5. Questionnaire on strengths and weaknesses

Think about what you can do or cannot do in the foreign language. (For example: talking with another student, filling in grammar tests, speaking without grammar mistakes, writing without grammar mistakes or spelling mistakes, understanding tape recorded speech, speaking in front of the whole class, speaking with correct pronunciation.) Finish the sentences below giving more than one example if you can.

In the foreign language, I am quite good at ....

In the foreign language, I am fairly good at ....

In the foreign language, I am not so good at ....

In the foreign language, I find it difficult to ....

Is there anything that you are good at, but still keen to improve, or anything that you find difficult, but you don't mind that much? Would you like to add any other comments?
....
....

© Cambridge University Press 2000

Writing a composition
writing about personal views or experiences

Main goal   collecting information on students' past experiences
Language focus   writing a report or expressing an opinion

If you feel you would like to learn about something in more detail, you can ask students to write a composition on the subject for homework. For example, to learn about the general classroom atmosphere you may have students write about how they would describe a swot (that is, someone disliked by the others because he or she studies 'too much'). Or, to find out about past experiences and feelings about certain teaching techniques, ask them what they liked or disliked about their previous teacher (unless of course you fear that it may embarrass the previous teacher or any other person in the school). By asking students about why they like or dislike learning the target language, you can learn a lot about their motivation (or the lack of it).

Giving feedback
giving feedback on new activities

Main goal   collecting information on students' reactions
Language focus   reading comprehension
Preparation   handouts

You may experiment with testing your students' reactions. If there is something new (a textbook, a game, or an activity) you want to try, you can go ahead and try it and then analyse the feedback you get from your learners. You may use questions like the ones below.

Did you enjoy using . . . . / doing the . . . . activity?
Did you feel you learnt more than usual with . . . . ?
Would you like to use/do . . . . again?
Do you have any suggestions for other ways to use . . . / improve the activity?
What did you feel most interesting or challenging about the new material/activity?
. . . .
What did you find unusual/boring about the new material/activity?
. . . .

Interviews
interviewing group mates on their learning preferences

Main goal	collecting information on preferred teaching styles and techniques
Language focus	oral fluency practice, *should/would*
Preparation	handouts

Present the following questions to your students. Elicit some answers to make sure that they understand all of them, and ask them if they can think of any other relevant questions. Then allocate the questions and ask students to interview each other and collect as many answers as they can. You may then collect and analyse their answers, and give them a summary of the results in the next lesson.

Interview questions

How would you like to work in class? (on your own, with a pair, in a group)
What sort of learning material would you like to work with? (textbooks, music, newspapers, magazines, books, videos, tape recordings, authentic or teaching material, etc.)
   What sorts of activities would you like to do in class? (drills, games, projects, etc.)
   Who should lead the activities? (the teacher, another student, you)
   How would you like your work to be evaluated? (in words, in marks, only by the teacher, each assignment or once a month/semester, etc.)
   How would you like to be corrected? (not at all, when you make a mistake, addressed to you, later, addressed to the class in general, only in written work, etc.)

© Cambridge University Press 2000

Group discussions
comparing likes and dislikes in learning

Main goal	collecting information on learner preferences
Language focus	oral fluency practice, writing a report, *like* with gerund
Preparation	(handouts)

Students work in groups to compare their likes, dislikes, and abilities in learning the foreign language. You may need to ask one student in each group to lead the discussion. If this role is new to the students, you may give one student in each group a role card entitled 'Group leader' like the one below:

Group leader

You will lead the discussion in this group.

- Make sure that everybody in the group has a chance to say what they think, and that nobody talks too much.
- Be polite but firm.
- If nobody is willing to speak, say what you think and ask some very easy questions.

You may write the questions to be discussed on the blackboard or give handouts to the groups. Give them some 10–15 minutes to talk and ask them to produce a short report. If necessary, you can also supply the patterns to be used in the report. So, the handout might look like this:

Discuss similarities and differences in the group in the following areas. Before you start, choose a secretary to take notes, and a chairperson to lead the discussion.

- types of class activities that you like best (dialogues in pairs, reading stories, listening to stories, doing grammar tests, etc.)
- your favourite sense (reading texts, watching pictures/video, listening to speech, listening to music, touching, miming)
- your best talent in the foreign language
- ways you use the foreign language outside class (friends, computer games, newspapers, holiday, etc.)

When you finish the discussion, write a report about the group as a whole.
You can start your sentences like this:
Most of us . . .
Some of us . . .
Not one of us . . .

© Cambridge University Press 2000

2.1.2 **Motivation**

First words
teaching and learning some internationally used words

Level	beginner/elementary
Main goal	self-confidence
Language focus	vocabulary building
Preparation	pictures or objects
Note	this activity is fairly short but spreads over two lessons

The point of this activity is to show students how much they already know, to mobilise their existing knowledge, and to encourage their contribution to classroom work.

In one of your first lessons with the group, for homework ask your students to find words that they already know, and find a way to teach them to or share them with the others (e.g. by miming them, or bringing a picture of them). Encourage them to choose words they think are unknown to the others – although students will also profit from relearning familiar words as they can confirm their correct pronunciation and spelling in the target language.

You may demonstrate the task before assigning it as homework. Bring a few objects or pictures of objects that your students are likely to know in the foreign language (in the case of English, such words may include cigarettes, a radio, a window), show them the objects and simply say their names, and perhaps write them on the blackboard.

In the next lesson, students will teach each other their chosen words – the whole class, or in groups of five to ten students. Ask a student (or a delegate from each group) to put the words on the blackboard so that they can see how much they know already. (You may need to teach *'nothing'* to students who did not do their homework!)

Variation 1:
At the end of a lesson ask students how many *verbs* they know in the foreign language and ask them to think about the answer at home. At the start of the next lesson ask the same question. Mime a simple verb and have the learners guess what it is. Collect all guesses on the blackboard, then mime another one or ask a student to carry on. Keep on with the activity until the list is long enough to be an encouragement for all the students. (Most of them are likely to make low estimates of their vocabulary.) If you think that miming would take too much time, you can simply have students brainstorm all the verbs they know.

Variation 2:
Instead of verbs, you can ask students to think of words in their mother tongue that are the same (or similar) in the foreign language.

Guessing hidden strengths
talking about special skills in the group

Level	elementary/intermediate
Main goals	self-confidence, group cohesion
Language focus	gerund forms, short answers
Notes	works well as a warm-up for groups of up to 15, use carefully if the local culture discourages self-praise, and use only with groups that have been together for a few weeks at least

The point here is to give confidence to the students and give them a chance to win the respect of the others in the group.

Ask students to write one sentence about themselves like this: *I am good at . . . -ing.* Tell them to choose a hidden strength that most others in the group do not know about. Collect all the sentences, shuffle them and give one to each student (make sure that nobody is given their own sentence). Ask students to try and guess who wrote the sentence they got, and read it out like this: *I think/suspect X is good at . . . -ing.* Then X can confirm if the statement applies, and if this was really the hidden strength (s)he wrote about. (To make this part easier for shy students, you can ask them either to just nod and smile or shake their head in response to the sentence.) You may need to intervene towards the end if there are students whom nobody mentioned. Just say 'Let me make a guess, too', and repeat one of the previously used sentences with the name of a neglected student. In a small class, you can let the guessing go on until students find the author of each sentence, while in a large class you can save time by limiting guesses to three and resolving any 'mysteries' at the end of the activity. For a more structured activity of this type see *The wallchart* (page 41). (Adapted from Davis and Rinvolucri, 1990.)

Out in the world
reporting on the use of the foreign language outside the classroom

Level	intermediate/advanced
Main goals	self-confidence, identifying difficulties
Language focus	reporting, written fluency practice, past tenses, reported speech
Note	may be used as a homework assignment

The activity reminds students of the ultimate aim of their learning, and gives them confidence as they recall an occasion when they had already put their knowledge to 'real' use. At the beginning of the school year, ask your students to think back to the summer, about an occasion when they used the foreign language in a real life situation (e.g. ordering a meal or asking for directions on holiday in a foreign country, or helping tourists in their own country). Ask them to write a report to you about the event, describing the circumstances, and also their personal interpretation: what was difficult, interesting or surprising for them, was there any feeling of success, etc. If some learners have no such personal experience, they can tell a family anecdote or one they read somewhere or saw on television. If there is a really good story, you may print it and use it for a reading activity in the next lesson.

Variation 1:
Alternatively, or as the next task, students can describe an event when they experienced some sort of difficulty in communicating.

Variation 2:
To boost their confidence, you can ask students to write the account of an occasion when they had a feeling of success in learning the foreign language, or when they enjoyed learning the foreign language in or outside the classroom. If you want to work on learning styles you may ask some students to tell their stories to the others as a lead-in to *My learning self* (page 43).

Troubles of the rich and famous
discussing the learning problems of a celebrity

Level	intermediate/advanced
Main goals	identifying difficulties, empathy
Language focus	describing, giving advice and suggestions, adjectives, *should/had better/ought to*
Preparation	handouts with short passage

The idea here is to get students to discuss learning problems without the embarrassment of having to talk about themselves.

You need a passage on some famous person (Mr/Ms X) describing his or her school days, and problems about learning. (See examples in the Appendix.) Preteach any words the students may find difficult, then ask them to read the story. Ask students to identify Mr/Ms X's characteristics as a learner. (If you find a suitable text, you may do this as a listening exercise, reading it to the students.) Ask students to work in pairs and, imagining that they are the parents of young Mr/Ms X, discuss how they could help or what they could do to get their child to improve in school performance.

You may use *Out in the world* (page 26) as a homework assignment after this activity. See *My learning self* (page 43) or *Sharing problems* (below) for a discussion of the students' own learning difficulties.

Variation:
Instead of a celebrity, you may use the problems of a person or fictional character who was less successful in life.

Sharing problems
discussing difficulties in learning the foreign language

Level	elementary/intermediate/advanced
Main goals	sharing personal experiences, identifying difficulties, empathy
Language focus	giving reassurance, rephrasing, *can/can't, so/nor do I*

Sympathetic listening is an important element of the activity as students are talking about their genuine problems. One way to emphasise this is to prepare role cards with clear instructions (see in the Appendix), as some students will not listen to instructions unless they are addressed specifically to them. Talking about such problems also helps increase awareness. You may need to preteach some expressions for giving a positive response.

Ask students to get into pairs. In each pair, one student talks about their problems in learning the foreign language, while the other listens attentively and sympathetically (using *so/nor do I*), and then tries to give reassurance. The easiest form of reassurance may be simply repeating or summarising in their own words what their partner has said. Students switch roles after four to five minutes.

As a follow up, you can ask some students if they shared any problems with their partner (an opportunity to teach *both*) or if there were any special/unusual problems. You can use *Troubles of the rich and famous* (page 27) to get students talking about problems in general, *My learning self* (page 43) for a discussion of both strengths and weaknesses, and Variation 2 for *Out in the world* (page 26) as follow up to counterbalance the negative tone of the activity.

2.1.3 Learning strategies

Pastimes
comparing favourite pastimes to learning preferences

Level   elementary/intermediate/advanced
Main goal   discovering learning styles
Language focus comparing, expressing preferences using *prefer/like doing something*, comparative adjectives

Ask students to think about how they like to spend their free time, and to make a list of favourite activities. Have pairs or groups share notes, and arrange the activities into groups under the following headings: picture, sound, movement, and touch. (Groups may overlap.) Ask them to check which group(s) their favourite pastimes tend to belong to. Explain that the categories they used correspond to the four main types of perception (see note for *Questionnaire on learning styles* on page 18). To clarify what this means in practice, you may put the four types on the blackboard and ask students how they could do a learning task (e.g. memorising irregular verb forms, or presenting a story for the class) in different ways corresponding to the four types. Then, ask them to think of their preferred type of perception when they learn things, e.g. do they read aloud or silently, or do they learn words by writing them down, and see if it is in the same group as their favourite pastimes. For example, Anita did pantomime for a few years and she is a devoted theatregoer: she remembers words best if she writes them down several times. So, it seems that for her *picture* and *movement* are more important than *sound*.

Forgetful me
analysing memories

Level   intermediate/advanced
Main goals   memory techniques, sharing personal experiences
Language focus *remember* + gerund, *can/can't*

This activity reveals differences in the way individuals remember things and helps students identify their strengths for themselves.

Ask students to recall events, names, places, smells, feelings, and sounds from their lives about five to ten years ago. They should list things they can remember and try and explain why they can remember these and not other things. Give them a few examples of your own memories. When they have five or six items on the list, they share it with their partner or in a small group and discuss the types of things they remember better, and how they could use this in learning new vocabulary.

Here is one example: we tried to recall the first time we talked about the idea of this book in 1994, four years later. Anita remembered that we were sitting in the cosy armchairs of Ágota's living room, and she felt comfortable and interested in our conversation. Ágota remembered that there was a freshness in the air as the door to the balcony was open, and the room was lit by the early afternoon sun. As it seems, Anita tends to remember feelings while Ágota often remembers smells and places. So Anita tries to associate new words with human characteristics, or to her own feelings about them (funny words always stick in her mind!), and Ágota links words to the situations in which she learnt them or where she could use them.

Grouping words
learning new words

Main goal   memory techniques
Language focus   vocabulary building
Preparation   (copies of word lists)

This activity introduces a technique for learning new words. On the blackboard, write a list of words you think are new to the class. It should be a random collection, with no grammatical or topical cohesion. Ask learners to look at the list and try to memorise as many of the words as they can in, say, five minutes. Then, erase the words and ask them to write down as many as they can remember. Do a quick survey to check results. Then, give them another list where the same number of new words are grouped in some logical way, and give them the same task. Check results and compare them with the first one. Explain that, in theory, learners should do better on the second task, as the meaningful grouping of words helps retention. If this was not the case, discuss what other factors may have helped them in doing the first task. Ask students what other techniques they know of and use for learning new words.

For more practice, you may give them the first list on a handout and ask them to try and group the words and learn them for the next lesson. You can check results next time.

Words for feelings
learning new words

Level	elementary/intermediate
Main goal	memory techniques
Language focus	vocabulary building, describing
Note	may use as a warm-up + round-off

This activity introduces a learning style and shows how it works in learning new words.

Start the lesson by writing two words on the blackboard expressing extremes of physical or mental state, such as: *tired/fresh, exhausted/energetic,* or *indifferent/excited.* Elicit words that describe states between the extremes and add one or two new words as well. Ask the students to write down and/or say a few sentences describing how they feel at the moment (e.g. *I am not very tired. I feel fit,* etc.), and encourage them to use the new words (e.g. ask if there is anyone who feels . . .). Then move on to some other activity. Before the end of the lesson, ask students to recall the new words they learnt at the beginning of the lesson. Ask if their mood has changed since then, and whether the new words were easy to remember. Explain that some people learn best if they link new input to movement or sensations, and associating new words with their own physical/mental state can help them remember words. Discuss how students could use this in practice, and then make a quick survey of who thought the technique could be useful.

Tuning in
identifying difficulties in listening

Level	intermediate/advanced
Main goals	focused listening, identifying difficulties
Language focus	stress, intonation, pronunciation
Preparation	tape recorded speech or dialogue (from textbook)

This activity helps students distinguish their problems with listening. Also, setting a double task may help some students to focus their attention better.

Before asking your students to do a listening exercise from the main textbook, write the following points (or those appropriate to the selection) on the blackboard:

- distractions
- speech too fast
- strange dialect
- too many new words
- background noise
- too much information

Check if they understand all the words, and have students copy the list of problems. Then ask them to do the listening task. Play the recording a second time and tell the learners that, whenever they find it difficult to follow the material, they should mark one of the reasons in the above list. At the end of the recording check how much they have understood, and ask which problems were marked most often. You may follow with a discussion on which of the problems are easier to deal with, and what can be done about them.

You may use *Why don't you listen?* (page 39) as lead-in for this activity.

Variation:
Rather than writing the problems on the blackboard yourself, invite the learners to cite problems they have had and build up the list together.

Singing story
catching key words in a song

Level	elementary/intermediate/advanced
Main goals	focused listening, guessing, self-confidence
Language focus	written fluency practice, vocabulary review
Preparation	tape recorded song + lyrics on handout or OHP
Note	may spread over two lessons or take up most of one lesson

This activity gives the learners some orientation and interest for listening without the tension of having to understand everything. It also helps them realise how much they can guess from understanding just a few words.

Select a pop song that has some story in it and for which you have the lyrics as well. Pick some key words from the song and write them on the blackboard.

Ask students how much they usually understand of the words of pop songs, and what clues they use (such as the title and the refrain). Then invite them to read the key words from the song and make up a story from them. (This could be done in writing, as a homework assignment.) Then play them the song and ask them to focus on two things: if the tunes matched their story at all, and whether they could recognise any of the key words. You may play the recording twice and then check how much they understood the story. Ask students whether having the key words helped them understand the whole story.

Finally, give them the lyrics, or read the story for them (simplify if necessary) so that they can compare it with their own. Discuss how much they could guess, and whether they can recognise and use key words in other tasks.

See *Weather forecast* (below) for a similar activity designed to introduce focused reading.

Weather forecast
reading for key words

Level	beginner/elementary/intermediate/(advanced)
Main goals	scanning, self-confidence
Language focus	vocabulary review, future forms
Preparation	handouts with weather forecast page from a daily/weekly paper or recorded from radio news in the foreign language

This activity introduces the idea of focused reading and helps students realise how much they can gather from just a few words.

You may use this activity to review vocabulary on weather conditions. Give students or pairs a copy of the weather forecast page of a foreign language paper: select a text which is well above the level of the group. Ask them to underline the words that they think describe the weather. When they have finished, ask them what they can say about the weather in the foreign country. Put a stroke on the blackboard for each idea or characteristic, and congratulate students on the amount they understood just by focusing on a few words! To prepare students for the idea of focusing, you may use *Singing story* (page 32), the listening version of this activity.

Variation 1:
With intermediate students, you may either set a tight time limit to make the task more difficult, or instead of reading, have them listen to the forecast (read it for them, or play recorded material).

Variation 2:
With intermediate and advanced students you may use any article suitable in content and length for the class. Distribute handouts and tell students to read through the text quickly and underline the words they know (other than articles and prepositions). Tell them that they have

only five minutes to do this. Next, they should reread the words they picked and then read the first paragraph more carefully. Ask them to try and guess what the article was about and exchange their interpretations with a partner. Then pool all guesses and see how close they are to each other and to the correct answer: point out to students that they were able to make good guesses without reading the whole article. For further practice, see *Reading assignment* on page 74.

Attentive reading
experimenting with reading strategies

Level	elementary/intermediate/advanced
Main goals	comprehension strategies, focusing on the learning process
Language focus	reading practice
Preparation	handouts
Note	may be used as a homework assignment

The aim of this activity is to get students to realise that different types of text require different modes of reading.

Select two written passages appropriate to the level of the students. They should be of about equal length and difficulty, but one of them should be a description of a person, a building or a landscape, elaborated with a lot of detailed information, and the other should be an interesting story, with a clear line of events. Give both to students and ask them to read each text only once as homework. They should write down the exact times when they started and finished reading and answer the questions below. Write these on the blackboard and ask students to copy them, so that they know what information to focus on when they are reading the text.

1 What is the main topic of the text?
2 Who is/are the main character(s)? (or, what is described in the text?)
3 Write down as many names and words as you can remember from the text.

In the next lesson check the answers to the first two questions. Have students compare reading times, level of comprehension and retention for the two texts, and discuss possible reasons for differences. You may start the discussion by asking students to estimate the time it would take to read *War and Peace* (or any other novel that they are likely to have heard of) and the time it would take to find out from a timetable when the next train leaves for London (or any other city relevant to the students). This is of course an exaggerated contrast between two different reading strategies, but it may help students realise that they do use different strategies in their reading, and that these very much depend on the nature of the particular task. For further practice in reading strategies, see *Reading assignment* on page 74.

Variation:
With advanced students you may use more difficult texts, and instead of the reading times, ask students to record the number of times they had to read the texts in order to be able to answer the comprehension questions.

How to read
experimenting with reading strategies

Level	intermediate/advanced
Main goals	scanning, skimming
Language focus	reading practice
Preparation	handouts with task sheet and written passage

The activity helps students realise that different reading tasks require different strategies in reading.

Select a written passage appropriate to the level of the class. Give each student the same passage but different task sheets to one half than to the other. The first task sheet should instruct students to look for specific pieces of information in the text, e.g. the name and occupation of characters or if there are any animals mentioned, etc. The second sheet should ask general comprehension questions that require careful reading of the whole text. The number of questions should be about the same. Give students the task sheet first and ask them to read it carefully before they set about the task. Then give them the text: they should read it only once, and *time* their reading.

Students in the first group are likely to finish earlier, so you may give some extra follow-up task at the bottom of the sheet that does not require further reading (e.g. make a list of animal names you know in the foreign language). When both groups have finished, have them compare reading times, and reveal the difference in their tasks. Discuss implications for reading strategy. For further practice in reading strategies, see *Reading assignment* on page 74.

How to guess
making and adjusting guesses

Main goals	guessing from clues, creativity
Language focus	vocabulary building
Preparation	handouts

Raising awareness

This activity invites students to stretch their minds and introduces a technique to get round unfamiliar words.

Select a passage appropriate to the level of the class, and make a list of the new words separate from the original text. Give students the list and ask them to make guesses on the meaning and grammatical type (noun, verb, etc.) of each word. Then give them the passage and have them adjust their guesses. Follow with a discussion on how and why they made adjustments and how they could use guessing in other tasks. For further practice in guessing from clues, see *Reading assignment* on page 74.

Facetalking
guessing words from facial expression and gestures

Main goals	communication strategies: using mimes and gestures, guessing from clues
Language focus	adjectives, vocabulary review
Preparation	cards
Note	this activity may not work out well with very shy or too lively groups

This activity helps students to realise how much they can express without words.

You will need stacks of cards with one adjective on each describing a person's physical or emotional state (e.g. *bored, tired, happy, sad, hurt, surprised, dreamy, sleepy, hot, cold*: see cards in the Appendix). Each pair or group gets a stack of cards, and one student picks up the first card (without showing it to anyone else!) and tries to mime the given emotional state by facial expression and gestures. The student who comes close enough (e.g. saying *tired* for *exhausted*) in guessing, takes up the next card. You may stop them after five minutes and see who acted or guessed best, and how many cards were used. As a follow up, discuss the difficulty of the task. Once students get to know the activity, you can invite them to add to the card collection. For further practice, see *Cartoon story* on page 61.

Variation:
Give each group a mask that covers the eyes and/or the face. Ask one learner from each group to put on the mask and try to express a feeling with body movements (you may let them choose for themselves) that others in the group will try to guess.

The other side
listening to an L2 speaker of the students' mother tongue

Main goals	communication strategies, self-confidence
Preparation	tape recording or printed text on handouts or OHP
Note	only works with monolingual groups

The activity focuses on the relationship between correct speech and communication, and gives confidence to the students by showing that they too can express a lot of ideas at their current level of accuracy.

Ask a native speaker of the foreign language to speak or write something (preferably matching some topic in the textbook) in the students' mother tongue, and record the performance, which should not be too proficient. Present the material to the students and ask them how much they understand, if they notice any mistakes, which mistakes hinder understanding most, etc. Discuss how much of the speaker's message got through despite the mistakes and whether this usually applies to their use of the foreign language as well. It may also be useful to discuss how students feel about making mistakes. With beginners, the follow-up discussion may be conducted in their mother tongue.

Variation:
With advanced students you may do a similar activity with some authentic material: unedited, natural native speech or transcript of speech in the foreign language. You can then focus on slips of grammar, halts and hesitation, search for words, etc. In another application, you may use the activity to focus on compensation strategies (using synonyms, circumlocution, etc.).

Just a smile
solving a simple situation in a one-sided conversation

Main goals	communication strategies: using mimes and gestures
Language focus	oral fluency practice, reported speech
Preparation	role cards

The point of the activity is to give students confidence in their communicative abilities, and show them a technique that helps them to communicate.

You need to prepare this activity with some discussion on mimes and gestures, or introduce the idea with another activity, such as *Facetalking* (page 36). Then students form pairs to act out a simple situation (see in the Appendix) with one of them speaking and the other one responding only with gestures and mimes. Partners switch roles after two to three minutes, and do another situation. After the activity, ask some students what their silent partner 'said' in their 'conversation'.

2.1.4 Community building

Who said what
learning students' names

Level	intermediate
Main goal	group cohesion
Language focus	reported speech
Note	may be especially useful in adult education

This activity encourages students to recognise others in the group (and not focus solely on the teacher).

In the first few weeks, after a group activity or pair work, ask a few students to report what the other(s) have said, mentioning the names as well, so that you can learn their names. It is of course also for the students to learn each other's names, which can be a first step towards cooperation and forming a community.

Close your ears
speaking without interruption and listening in pairs

Level	elementary/intermediate/advanced
Main goals	sharing personal experiences, empathy
Language focus	oral fluency practice
Preparation	role cards A and B (see in the Appendix)
Note	may take a long time if students get interested in the discussion part

This activity helps students realise the significance of being attentive and giving feedback in communication.

Students work in pairs. In each pair, give one student role card A or ask them to think of a serious problem they would like to tell somebody about, and give card B to the other student. The role of A is to share a problem with a friend and the role of B is to be an uninterested, unsympathetic listener. Partners take turns in the two roles, and when they finish they discuss the experience. Most students will note that it was not nice to speak to an inattentive audience. Get them to describe the behaviour of bad listeners and the reasons why this may disturb the speaker.

The experience may create a bad feeling in some, so it is useful to follow with a more pleasant activity, such as *Just a smile* (page 37), or the same dialogues with a different card B (see in the Appendix).

Why don't you listen?
speaking without interruption and listening in pairs

Level	intermediate/advanced
Main goals	sharing personal experiences, cooperation
Language focus	oral fluency practice

The activity builds trust between students, and it may also make students think consciously about the difficulties they have when listening to somebody talking.

Pair students and ask A to speak for ninety seconds about a topic chosen by B, and accepted by A as well. While A talks, B makes a mark on a piece of paper every time they are distracted from listening to A. (This could be a background noise, a train of thought invoked by A's speech or a totally unconnected own thought.) Repeat with reverse roles. When both partners have had their turn, they each report to the whole class (or to a group of six or seven) one thing from what the other has said. At the end, ask students what sort of distractions they had, and what was difficult/easy about the task. You may use this activity as a lead-in to *Tuning in* (page 31).

Variation:
You may ask the speaker to think of three feedback questions to ask from the listener and then report how many were answered correctly.

Two in the bush
analysing cooperation in pair work

Level	elementary/intermediate
Main goal	cooperation
Language focus	giving suggestions, asking for feedback, expressing likes and dislikes
Note	may not work in classes with discipline problems

Ask students to work together in pairs and draw a dog or a house: something not too complex or difficult, but not too simple either. (Your choice may depend on how you want to continue after the activity.) There is one important rule: the students must not use their native language while they are drawing; they can only communicate in the foreign language. When they finish, ask them to think about *how* they worked together. If necessary, you may write some very specific questions on the blackboard that they can discuss, such as:

Did one of you work more than the other on the drawing?
Did one of you dominate decisions about what to draw and how?
Did you take turns in adding to the picture?
Did you look at or ask your partner for feedback (approval/disapproval)?
Do you think that you could have produced a better picture on your own?
Did you feel comfortable/irritated while working together?

If you find that students felt irritated by the exercise, get them to focus on the positive side: ask them if they experienced anything interesting, if they liked anything in their partner's contribution, or if they got any new ideas about how to draw. For cooperation in group work, see the variation or *Group work analysis* (below).

Variation:
Do any exercise from the main textbook that involves students working in groups, e.g. writing a story together. When this is finished, ask them to think about how they worked together. If necessary, you may write the questions above (or similar ones) on the blackboard for them to discuss.

Group work analysis
discussing roles in group work

Level	elementary/intermediate/advanced
Main goals	group cohesion, cooperation
Language focus	reporting, simple past

The point of this activity is to make students think about working as a group.

As a follow up to an activity that involved loosely structured group work, ask students to put a number as an answer to the following (or similar) questions, as appropriate to the task:

How many people are there in the group?
During the previous activity how many of them
- spoke only in the foreign language?
- took notes or wrote things down?
- asked questions connected to the activity?
- answered some questions connected to the activity?
- made suggestions connected to the activity?
- invited someone else in the group to contribute?

© Cambridge University Press 2000

Ask students which question got the lowest and the highest figure as an answer. On the blackboard, fill in a chart for the class. In the figures row write fractions, using the total number of group members as the denominator, so the chart may look like this:

		lowest	highest
group 1 (5 students)	Did what?	took notes	spoke only the foreign language
	How many students?	$\frac{1}{5}$	$\frac{4}{5}$
group 2 (6 students)	Did what?	made suggestions	answered questions
	How many students?	$\frac{0}{6}$	$\frac{4}{6}$
group 3 (6 students)	Did what?	made suggestions	took notes
	How many students?	$\frac{1}{6}$	$\frac{5}{6}$

Follow with a discussion on why these actions are important in group work and whether students thought they would need more or less of any of these when they work in a group next time. However, do not expect much improvement after the exercise: it takes a lot more to change existing routines and attitudes. For further practice, see also *Working as a group* on page 71.

The wallchart
learning about group mates' tastes and skills in learning

Level	intermediate/advanced
Main goals	group cohesion, discovering learning styles
Language focus	brief, neat writing for display
Preparation	large piece of cardboard, blank sheets of paper, and glue or blu-tack

This activity helps students think consciously about themselves as learners and realise that others may be different, while they may also discover shared tastes or interests. Also, it encourages them to think of the class as a community.

Use questionnaires, group discussion, interviews, or other techniques (see examples on pages 18–24) to collect information about the students, so that they can prepare a wallchart with the following headings:

NAME	FAVOURITE CLASS ACTIVITIES	FAVOURITE SENSE (EYES, EARS, ETC.)	BEST TALENT IN THE FOREIGN LANGUAGE	USES THE FOREIGN LANGUAGE OUTSIDE CLASS IN:

If the class likes the idea, you may display the chart in the classroom. From time to time you may want to go back to this activity and amend the chart as necessary.

Splitting up
looking for similarities and differences between objects and people

Level	intermediate/advanced
Main goal	sharing personal experiences
Language focus	comparing, expressing feelings and preferences, reporting, adjectives
Note	may be used to dismantle early tendencies towards the formation of cliques in the class

This activity gives students a chance to realise that they may have things in common with any group mate, not only with their friends.

Draw the above five shapes on the blackboard and ask learners to arrange them into two groups (two in one and three in the other) according to similarities and differences. One and four solutions are not acceptable!

Have some students explain their solution at the blackboard. Next, divide the class into groups of five or six and then ask them to split into two subgroups each, as they did with the shapes. Ask them to report to the whole class their solutions and the reasons behind them. You may use the new groups in the next activity.

2.1.5 **Self-monitoring**

My learning self
comparing personalities in and outside the classroom

Level	intermediate/advanced
Main goal	focusing on the learning process
Language focus	describing people, adjectives, simple present
Preparation	list of adjectives on OHP or blackboard

This activity helps students think consciously about themselves as learners.

Make up a list of adjectives that may describe people as language learners (e.g. *slow, careful, lazy, serious, friendly, shy, talkative, interested, enthusiastic, passive, quick, diligent, impatient, careless, thorough, forgetful, discouraged, active, attentive, playful* – try as much as possible to avoid any reference to values attached to the adjectives!) and display it for the class to see. Encourage students to add to the list and then ask them to pick the words they feel best characterise them. Ask them to work in pairs and discuss if these characteristics are true for their personalities in general, or only in language learning. They can also think about which ones help their learning and which do not.

You may use the list of adjectives in the next activity to teach word formation: the use of suffixes and prefixes in forming adjectives.

Learning styles
discovering differences in learning styles

Level	elementary/intermediate
Main goals	discovering learning styles, group cohesion
Language focus	adverbs of time and frequency, collective pronouns
Note	may take up half or all of the lesson

Sometimes students tend to assume that everybody else learns the same way as they do. This activity makes them realise that this is not the case, and helps them to think consciously about possible learner characteristics. Also, learning about each other fosters group cohesion.

Ask students to get into groups of two or three and make sentences about their learning routines and characteristics, either true or false, using the following pattern: *We always / sometimes / . . . / never . . .* , (e.g. *When learning new words, we always read them aloud*, or *We never ask for help from our parents*). When ready, they read the ones they like best to the whole class, who will guess which are true and which are false.

Follow with a discussion on differences in the class: you may start this by asking students if they had learnt anything surprising about each other during the activity. See also *The wallchart* (page 41) for a further development of this activity.

Variation 1:
You may ask pairs to write sentences about themselves (things that are true or untrue) and then read a few of these to the whole class. The class then decides how much these characterise the class as a whole.

Variation 2:
To help develop group cohesion, you may use this activity with some other topic, e.g. hobbies, interests, personal characteristics, family members. You may also change and extend the patterns provided. Thus, for example to practise the present perfect tense, students will write sentences like *We have all been to New York.* or *None of us has seen an octopus.*

Favourite activities
comparing preferences in language learning

Level	elementary/intermediate/advanced
Main goal	discovering learning styles
Language focus	reporting
Preparation	handouts with questionnaire
Note	may take up half or all of a lesson

The idea here is to help students realise that members of the group may have different preferences, and to get them to think of reasons behind their own likes and dislikes.

Prepare a questionnaire on what types of classroom activities students like best (see pages 18 and 23 for some ideas). Explain to students that you would like to know how they like to learn, so that you can make the lessons more effective, and ask them to fill in the questionnaire individually. Then, they get into groups and compare their tastes and try to explain their preferences. Ask each group to report one activity they all like, and one that they have mixed feelings about. If they can, they should explain the reasons behind their choices. Once the groups have finished, collect questionnaires for later analysis. You may use *My learning self* (page 43) as a lead-in to this activity.

Variation 1:
If you have used *My learning self* as a lead-in, you may ask students to work in pairs/groups corresponding to their adjectives, and see if their characteristics correspond to their tastes in classroom activities.

Variation 2:
You may use this variation some time later, when students have had more experience in thinking about classroom work. Ask students to think over the activities done in class over some period (that lesson, day, week, etc.). Using what they recall, make a list on the blackboard (in a large class, groups work together to compile the list), and then ask them to decide (either individually or in small groups)

- how much they liked the activity
- how useful they found the activity
- why it was useful (what they practised, gained) or not useful, and
- how it could be improved.

Follow with a discussion with the whole class, or in groups in the case of a large class. (See also *What's the point?* on page 77.)

How do I learn words?
writing a brief report

Level	elementary/intermediate/advanced
Main goal	focusing on the learning process
Language focus	past tenses, reporting
Note	may be used as a homework assignment

Along with an assignment to learn a list of words, ask learners to write a short passage on how they set about the task. You may need to tell them what exactly you are interested in. For example, you may ask about the amount of time they spent on studying, if they read the words silently or aloud, if they asked someone to practise with them, if they took notes on the meanings and in what language, if they wrote down the new words one by one, or in sentences, etc. You may continue with *Ways to words* after this activity.

Ways to words
trying new techniques to learn words

Main goal	focusing on the learning process
Language focus	vocabulary building, gerund or simple present
Note	takes some courage both from the teacher and the students

Ask students how they usually learn new words: most likely, they will come up with different strategies. Ask them to think of other possible ways, and give them a few examples of your own (such as arranging words into categories, putting sticky labels on objects in their room, or trying to use new words as often as they can). Then let them try one or two new strategies: give out a list of words (10–15 items) and ask students to memorise them using a new strategy of their choice (feasible in the given environment). Allow some time to discuss how they liked the experience, and whether they thought the new method could be better than their old ways. You may use *My learning self* (page 43) or *How do I learn words?* (page 45) as a lead-in to this activity.

Further reading

Bialystok, Ellen and Hakuta, Kenji (1994) *In Other Words: The Science and Psychology of Second Language Acquisition*, Basic Books, Harper and Collins describes cognitive styles in various dimensions (such as ambiguity tolerance, or reflectivity versus impulsiveness).

Christison, Mary Ann and Bassano, Sharron (1987) *Purple Cows and Potato Chips*, Prentice Hall is a collection of activities, including some inspiring ideas on how to use multi-sensory activities in language learning.

Cohen, Andrew D. (1998) *Strategies in Learning and Using a Second Language*, Longman discusses the importance of awareness in using strategies and the advantages of explicit strategy training. The author also reports the results of a strategy training project, and provides some practical ideas.

Ehrman, Madeline E. (1996) *Understanding Second Language Learning Difficulties*, Sage Publications offers ideas on collecting information on the learner, and some practical advice on how to deal with individual differences in learning styles.

Ellis, Gail and Sinclair, Barbara (1989) *Learning to Learn English*, Cambridge University Press offers step by step training for responsibility mostly focusing on learning skills and the cognitive involvement of students.

Hadfield, Jill (1992) *Classroom Dynamics*, Oxford University Press offers activities for thinking about the language, groups, and individual learning styles, as well as some empathy activities, some to ensure participation, on learning to listen, classroom interaction, and discipline problems.

Lawlor, Michael (1988) *Inner Track Learning*, Pilgrims describes techniques to bring right brain hemisphere faculties into the learning process: some may be useful for building awareness.

Oxford, Rebecca (1990) *Language Learning Strategies*, Heinle and Heinle Publishers suggests some ideas for assessing the existing strategies of your students.

Reid, Joy M. (1995) *Learning Styles in the English as a Second Language Classroom*, Heinle and Heinle Publishers gives some practical ideas on how to accommodate teaching to particular styles. The chapters on visual, auditory and kinaesthetic learners may be especially useful for building awareness.

Rinvolucri, Mario (1982) *Awareness activities for teaching structures*, in Humanistic Approaches, ELT Documents 113, The British Council, discusses different types of awareness activities and gives some examples.

Tarone, Elaine and Yule, George (1995) *Focus on the Language Learner: Approaches to Identifying and Meeting the Needs of Second Language Learners*, Oxford University Press provides practical ideas and some activities to identify learners' needs.

Willing, Ken (1989) *Teaching How to Learn, Learning Strategies in ESL*, National Centre for English Language Teaching and Research, Sidney, Macquarie University includes a discussion of learning styles and strategies, and some activities.

2.2 Changing attitudes

The activities in this section are designed to practise and habituate the attitudes and strategies introduced in the awareness raising exercises.

Most activities are based on the assumption that students are already aware of (i.e. they have consciously identified) the skill or attitude they are encouraged to practise. Also, the activities in this section are less tightly structured than those in the first section: they require more learner initiative and a higher level of responsibility. If you feel that your students do not have the necessary awareness or degree of responsibility, we recommend that you work a bit more on these areas, using activities in the first section. You may find some further sources for awareness raising activities at the back.

Just as in the previous section, activities are concerned with motivation, learning strategies, community building, and self-monitoring. The first group of activities serves to sustain the interest and self-confidence of the learner by stimulating their creativity and inviting them to use their personal experiences and non-language knowledge. This is crucial, as only motivated and confident students are likely to want to take charge of their learning.

Next, we present activities that help learners *consciously* practise learning strategies. It is very important that learners are aware of what strategies they apply while doing the tasks: you may ask them about this before they set out to work, and/or discuss it after the activity.

Activities in the third group develop cooperation and group cohesion. Most of them serve simply to practise cooperation without much discussion about how it actually takes place, as this was already covered in the previous section. Just *doing* pair and group work itself helps the development of responsible attitudes in many ways. It reduces the dominance of learner–teacher interaction, encourages students to rely on each other and on themselves, and spreads responsibility for the achievement of a task more evenly among students. Also, students learn to listen to and respond to each other: this is to prepare them for peer evaluation and peer-correction that we introduce in the next section.

The fourth group is concerned with self-monitoring: these activities invite students to be 'their own teachers' in two ways. For one thing, students identify and consider ways of dealing with their mistakes and problems in their learning. For another, they think about the aims and resources of their learning. There are two important aims here: students need to be conscious of how and why (or why not) they learn and do things, and they need to get used to regularly monitoring their own performance.

We recommend that you identify the areas where your students need development the most and then give them plenty of practice opportunities with an emphasis on these areas before moving on to the 'transferring roles' stage. Most of the activities in this section may be applied to different written or recorded materials and used several times. Some may even become a permanent part of classroom work. With many of the activities we have provided ideas for variations, and there is an annotated bibliography at the back that will help you find further materials and activities.

2.2.1 Motivation

Below you will find a small selection of activities to develop intrinsic motivation. If you wish to work more on this area, we recommend that you look for further sources of similar activities: we have included some in the bibliography.

Getting in the mood
getting ready to concentrate on the lesson

Main goals	creativity, sharing personal experiences
Language focus	describing, adjectives
Note	works well to ease tension or cheer up a tired group

If students look tired or tense at the beginning of or during a lesson, you may use this activity to ease some of the tension and create a more positive atmosphere. The activity reinforces the idea that concentration is essential for learning to take place.

Ask some students if they feel tired, sleepy, worried, if they have a headache, or any other problem that disturbs them. Then suggest that they do a quick exercise to refresh their minds. Ask everyone to close their eyes for a minute and concentrate on whatever problem they have, and try to visualise it as an object that has shape, size, colour, surface, etc. After a minute or so, ask students to get into pairs and take turns describing this object to each other. Finally, you may ask them to take an imaginary eraser and wipe out the object from their minds. To round it off, you may say something like: *Fine! I hope you can concentrate better on the lesson now.*

Variation:
As a follow up, you may ask students to make a list of feelings (states of the mind) that help or hinder learning.

Family morning
discussing daily activities at home

Level	elementary/intermediate
Main goals	sharing personal experiences, personalising new input
Language focus	present continuous, past continuous, (present perfect)

Creating a link with the students' personal experiences increases motivation and helps the retention of new vocabulary or grammatical patterns. This activity is an example of this, applied to practising the present continuous tense.

Ask students to think about the moment they left home in the morning, and recall what the members of their family were doing then. (They can use their imagination if they do not know exactly, and include the extended family if they have no brothers or sisters.) Recalling the moment as if they were still there, they should write three to five sentences in the present (continuous) tense. When they finish, allow a few minutes for any questions they may want to ask each other.

Next, you may ask pairs to read each other's writing, and then ask them what the family of their partner were doing when he/she left home. You may also ask if anyone wrote about an unusual activity. Put your questions in the past tense if you want students to practise the past continuous in their answers. If necessary, you may make this explicit before asking questions by writing *Now . . .* and *When he was about to leave . . .* on the blackboard. For another activity to practise the present continuous see *Time zones* (page 54).

Variation 1:
You may ask students to think of the activities of their family as a background to some strange or surprising event, and ask them to invent a story that could begin with the peaceful scene they described. (Something like this: *Dad was putting on his shoes, Katie was taking a shower, and Mum was drinking her coffee – when suddenly, ...*) You may ask them to write the first sentence (using the past continuous) in class, and finish the story for homework.

Variation 2:
To practise the past continuous, you may ask students what *they* were doing at a particular moment when something special happened. This can be any recent event that students were aware of, such as when election results were officially announced, news came of the assassination of a prominent politician, or public transport stopped due to a general strike.

Variation 3:
You may adapt the activity to other grammatical patterns. For example, to practise the present perfect, ask students to think of all the things they have accomplished since they got up in the morning, and make as many sentences as they can. They should think of the period up to the present moment as a whole, and thus use the present perfect tense. (Give a few examples if necessary.) When they have some eight to ten sentences, or at the end of the time limit you set, ask them to compare their sentences in pairs or in small groups. You can ask them to find as many similarities as they can, or select some sentences and ask each other about the details of the given activity. If they are working in groups, you can ask students to add up the number of all the things they have done, not counting duplicates.

Noah's ark
collecting favourite/important objects

Level	elementary/intermediate/advanced
Main goal	personalising input, sharing ideas
Language focus	expressing feelings and preferences, conditionals
Note	works best on a rainy day!

You may use this activity to give a personal touch to introducing a new topic.

Ask students if they remember Noah's story from the Bible. If necessary, elicit or give them a short account of the story. Ask students to think about three objects or things they would like to preserve (besides the animals) if they were in Noah's place. Limit the scope of their choice to suit your topic. For example, in a lesson about musical tastes students will select the best pieces of music. If the lesson is about their own country, they can think of objects, monuments, or special characteristics that they like about their homeland. Ask students to get into pairs or small groups and tell each other about their choices and considerations.

Adding a touch of colour
rewriting a story

Level	intermediate/advanced
Main goal	creativity
Language focus	written fluency practice, relative clauses
Preparation	handouts with a simple text

This activity provides a chance for creativity as well as focused practice in sentence construction.

Give students or pairs the handout with a text that contains short and simple sentences. (See *Simple story* in the Appendix.) Ask them to make the story cheerful, funny, sad, or mysterious, as they choose (perhaps to reflect their mood at the time), by inserting relative clauses wherever possible. If the task is unfamiliar, you may mark the points where this is possible, and give one or two examples, such as below:

A friend* invited me to a party*.
A friend, *who has just returned from a tour round the world*, invited me to a party. (excited, energetic)
A friend invited me to a party, *which was exactly on the day before my exam*. (sad, disappointed, or maybe bitter)

Let students work for at least five minutes. In a small class, ask students to read their version, and have the class decide how it strikes them. In a large class have pairs read each other's writing and comment on its tone.

Variation 1:
You may do a similar activity to practise adjectives, link words, or adverbs. With link words, you cannot really add any emotional touch, but you can increase cohesion, or perhaps play with changing the meaning of a text. See *Making ends meet* (page 66) for a possible lead-in.

Variation 2:
You may start from a sentence or a passage that contains 'neutral' words, and ask students to exaggerate it. For example, *Old Joe Smith likes to drink a pint in the evening* may evolve into **Ancient Joe Smith is only happy when guzzling beer all evening**.

Eiffel tower
choosing a colour to repaint a building

Level	elementary/intermediate/advanced
Main goals	self-confidence, creativity
Language focus	arguing and persuading, conditionals

As there are no wrong answers, this activity gives room for creativity and increases confidence.

Ask pairs to discuss what colour they would want to paint the Eiffel tower in Paris if they had the chance to decide. If students don't know the tower, choose some other building they are familiar with, e.g. their school. At the elementary level students may simply practise *would* in questions and answers, while advanced students can try their hands at persuasion techniques. After five minutes, in a small class you may just ask a few pairs about their decision and their reasons, or in a larger class form groups of four students and have them exchange their views. You may also collect 'votes' and then officially state the majority decision of the class.

Variation:
You may also ask students what other changes they would like to make to the building if they could (and had lots of money).

Spot the error
finding errors in public announcements

Level	intermediate/advanced
Main goals	self-confidence, communication strategies
Notes	for homework; may be useful to do *The other side* (page 37) before this activity

This activity emphasises the communicative function of language. Correcting mistakes in printed materials or public announcements may increase students' self-confidence, and lower their inhibitions about using the foreign language.

Ask students to look around the neighbourhood where they live and find signs, posters, and advertisements written in the foreign language (in the street, on public transport vehicles, in shops or offices, or in newspapers) and find as many mistakes as they can. They should take notes on their findings, and present them for correction in the class. You may discuss how the mistakes changed the message of the signs, or whether they created a problem at all. Also, you may ask students how they could use these signs in their learning.

Variation:
You may focus on grammar mistakes for revision, or a specific grammar area for more practice.

Time zones
comparing daily routines at different times and places

Level	beginner/elementary/intermediate
Main goals	creativity, bringing in outside knowledge, empathy
Language focus	written fluency practice, present continuous
Preparation	world map (with time zones)

This activity provides an unusual perspective and invites students to put to use the knowledge they have about different cultures and lifestyles.

Display a big world map (with time zones indicated if possible) and ask the students to choose a country (outside the continent where they live) they like or find interesting. Ask them to calculate the current time in this country and then imagine what people could be doing there at this time of the day. You may give them some examples, such as:

> People are going to work. They are sitting in their cars in a traffic jam, and they're listening to the news on the radio. Some of them are still drinking their morning coffee. (8 am in the US)
>
> People are at home, eating lunch. Or, they are just having a nap after lunch. Streets are empty: people are not shopping and they are not sitting in cafés because everything is closed for the siesta. (2 pm in Spain)

Students get five to ten minutes to write as many sentences as they can. As a follow up, ask some of them to read a few of their sentences and invite the class to guess the country or the time of the day. You may use *Family morning* (page 50) to introduce the vocabulary needed for this activity.

Variation 1:
You may ask the students to include some clues on the culture of the country of their choice in their sentences. In this variation they should write their sentences on a slip of paper and put on their names as well. Then you collect and shuffle their slips and distribute them again. Ask the students to read the sentences they get, try to guess the country, and return their answer to the author of the sentences.

Variation 2:
For the follow-up part, you can group students according to the zone they chose, and have them compile a list of the most unusual or interesting activities they collected or write a passage on how activities change from the North to the South, within the same zone. These could be read to the whole class.

2.2.2 Learning strategies

Listening for verb clues
listening in order to pick verbs

Main goals	focused listening, guessing from clues
Language focus	verb tenses
Preparation	recorded material (from textbook)

The point of this activity is that students listen for specific information without worrying about not understanding every detail. You may need to prepare your students for this activity with some awareness raising exercise (e.g. *Weather forecast* on page 33).

Ask students to listen to the recorded material and try to write down all the verbs *and only the verbs* they hear. With the more advanced you may want to focus solely on specific tenses, e.g. present perfect or past perfect forms.

Before they start, ask if they remember doing similar tasks that involved focusing on specific bits of information, and the aim of these tasks: this is to help them consciously prepare for focused listening. Then play the recording. Next, students may continue to work individually, or collect all the verbs that the material contains in pairs. Looking at the verbs they should try to reconstruct the situation or the story. Discuss ideas with the whole class. Elicit some solutions first and then play the recording again, asking students to try and understand the whole story now. Check how accurately they guessed on the basis of the verb lists. If the focus was on a particular verb tense, you may discuss how the situation determined the use of tenses.

Variation:
Instead of verbs, you can do the activity with adjectives or nouns.

Look and listen
telling a story in a group

Level	elementary/intermediate/advanced
Main goals	focused listening, personalising new input
Language focus	oral fluency practice, reported speech
Note	may be difficult to get it going for the first time

The set-up of the activity requires students to listen to each other as their performance depends on the others and they are called on randomly to take their turn. Each student is responsible for the outcome. However, building up a story together makes this arrangement a source of excitement rather than a threat.

Have the groups/class (five to nine people) sit in a circle and assign each person a number starting from one. Groups decide on the subject of the story they are going to tell. Explain the procedure: someone volunteers to start by saying a sentence and then calling a number: the person holding the number will continue. All the others must look at the one to speak, who will sum up what the previous person said (a good chance to use reported speech), add his or her own sentence, and then call the next number. And so on until the story is finished. Allow some time before and after the activity to discuss the aims of the task. (Adapted from Brandes and Ginnis, 1992.)

Associations
linking new words to old ones

Main goals	memory techniques, personalising new input, sharing ideas
Language focus	vocabulary review
Preparation	new words on the blackboard or on OHP
Note	may be used as a homework assignment

This activity provides practice and shows new ways of making associations when learning new words.

As a follow up for an activity that involved learning new words (e.g. reading a passage from the textbook), ask students to look at the new words and try to associate each with another word they already know. Look at for example, three words connected to ice:

icicle – bicycle (sounds similar)
frost – frozen (same topic, begins with same sound)
hail – storm (goes together in compound word)

When they finish, ask them to work in pairs (or small groups) and try to put their associations into categories, such as 'sounds similar', 'begins with same syllable', 'goes together in a phrase', 'similar meaning', 'similar topic', or any other they find suitable. Do not give too many examples as that may influence the students' own ideas too much. When each pair or group has covered most of the words, let them each explain one category to the whole class. You may then discuss how they use categories and associations in learning new words, and perhaps other memory techniques they can use.

Word families
grouping words

Main goals	memory techniques, personalising new input
Language focus	vocabulary review
Preparation	list of words on the blackboard or OHP

This activity is built on the idea that remembering words is easier if we link them to other words we already know. If your students are not aware of this memory technique, introduce the idea with an awareness raising activity (such as *Associations* on page 56).

Present a list of ten to twenty words on the blackboard that you would like to review (e.g. new words from the text students read in the previous lesson and some old ones connected to the same topic). Ask students to work in pairs or small groups and arrange the words into three or more categories, on any basis they find appropriate. They should give a name to each 'word family'.

When students have managed to sort out most of the words, ask for some of the category names, and have the rest of the class figure out which words it may contain. You may then discuss how students can use categories in learning or reviewing words. (Adapted from Willing, 1989.)

Pictures and words
linking words to pictures

Level	beginner/elementary/intermediate
Main goals	memory techniques, creativity
Language focus	vocabulary review
Preparation	as many pictures as groups

Concepts are easier to remember if we link them to an image: the activity provides practice in this technique.

Prepare some pictures each showing something different (people or objects) and neither too simple nor too complex, such as a family coming out of a house, a dog chasing a cat, a figure standing in the rain. Give one picture to each group and ask them to write down as many words about or connected to the picture as they can. Make it clear that this is not a free associations exercise: the purpose is to link words (concepts) to pictures. When they have some ten to fifteen words, or at the end of five minutes, groups exchange their photos. They will now use the same list they have compiled, and try to link the old words with the new picture. They can use all sorts of associations now. Look at the example overleaf:

The first picture may prompt the following associations: *alone, rain, cold, dark.* These words may be linked to the second picture like this:

    they are going to see Grandma who lives *alone*

    they are wearing boots because the soil is damp from the *rain*

    they are coming outside because it's *cold* and *dark* in the house

Discuss how they can use this technique when learning words, e.g. they can make a list of words they find difficult to remember, and try to link each with a picture (mental or real). Knowing about this technique may also help them choose study materials.

As a follow up, you may use the lists to practise word types: ask them to rewrite the lists grouping nouns or adjectives together. Alternatively, you may refer back to the pictures and check if students tended to write more verbs or nouns for particular photos and if so, why.

Going easy
describing the way people walk

Level	elementary/intermediate
Main goals	personalising new input, memory techniques
Language focus	adverbs, simple present
Preparation	cards with one adverb on each
Note	young learners especially are likely to enjoy this activity

Apart from giving a cheerful start to the lesson, this activity makes students think about usual things from a less obvious perspective. Such a remapping of ideas may create new associations and thus reinforce knowledge. The activity suits especially fidgety students – the restless type who can never stay still. (On this learning style see also *Words for feelings* on page 31.)

Prepare as many cards as students (there may be some duplicates) with instructions and adverbs that the students know or can easily guess. They should all apply to the manner of walking, e.g. *slowly*, *quickly*, *hurriedly*, *gracefully*, *pompously*, *carefully*, *hastily*, *noisily*, *clumsily*, *short-sightedly*, *cheerfully*, *sadly*, etc. The cards could look something like this (you only need to change the adverb in each):

> Please walk
> SLEEPILY to your
> desk. Sit down and
> watch as the
> others come in. Try
> to write down a
> word that
> describes the way
> they walk for each
> person.

Make sure that you arrive first at the classroom. Stand in the door, and give a card to everybody as they are coming in, asking them to read it before they move on, and follow the instructions on the card. When everybody has arrived, ask for some adverbs that the students noted down, and write them on the blackboard. It is probably best if you ask them how particular students walked in.

When you have some five or six adverbs on the blackboard, ask students to think about what things they usually do in such a manner. Ask them to write four to five sentences such as *I eat slowly*, *I dance clumsily*. Invite some students to read their sentences, and put some of the verbs they mention on the blackboard, connecting them to the appropriate adverb. Follow with a discussion on which links they find unusual, surprising, or perhaps funny, and explain how these unusual links may help the retention of words.

You may use the list of adverbs in some other activity, such as *Adding a touch of colour* (page 52), or to teach the rules of forming adverbs by adding suffixes.

Keys to spelling
finding spelling patterns in words

Level	elementary/intermediate
Main goal	generalising from examples
Language focus	spelling
Preparation	handouts with list of words

This activity is an example of inviting students to look for consistent spelling patterns in the foreign language so that they have a stable base, and can improve their performance without much increasing the load on their memories.

Give each group a list of words that follow the same rule of spelling. For example, in English you could use the following rules: *q* followed by *u*, double consonant in gerund form of monosyllable words as in *running*, or *-es* in the plural of some words like *glass*. Ask students to try and figure out the rule, and add some more examples if they can. (If you gave different lists to the different groups, have each group explain the rule to the others.) Ask them if they have ever used these rules consciously when writing in the foreign language.

Variation:
You may apply the activity to other structures, such as the use of prefixes and suffixes in word formation, pronunciation rules, or grammatical patterns. (See for example *Guessing grammar* on page 91.)

Idioms
making sense of idioms

Level	intermediate/advanced
Main goals	creativity, inferring
Language focus	vocabulary building
Preparation	idioms written on the blackboard or OHP
Note	may be used to introduce a topic

This activity broadens the students' perception of expressing ideas and shows that they can make sense of some idioms even when they hear them for the first time. The activity may work better if you have done some awareness raising exercise on guessing techniques (such as *How to guess* on page 35) beforehand.

You need a collection of idioms connected to a central theme, such as the following lists:

(romantic love)	(anger)	(money)
to carry a torch for someone	to lose one's temper	to be in the black
to break someone's heart	to make one's blood boil	to be short of
to think the world of someone	to blow/let off steam	to rake it in
to sweep someone off his feet	to make one's hackles rise	to make ends meet
to fall for someone	to raise hell	to give away/sell for a song
to pop the question	to fly off the handle	to make a mint

Display the idioms and ask students to try and figure out the concept they are all related to. Once they have found this key word, ask them to suggest possible meanings for the idioms. You do not have to cover all that is on the blackboard. In a large class, you may ask students to work in groups and write down their suggestions. Follow with a discussion on when to use idioms and how to understand them (e.g. by using the context, or generalising the literal meaning).

Cartoon story
adding words to a cartoon story

Level	elementary/intermediate/advanced
Main goals	guessing from clues, creativity, mimes and gestures, empathy
Language focus	written and oral fluency practice
Preparation	cartoons on handouts

This activity draws attention to the non-verbal clues we use in communication: you may use it to develop the skills introduced in *Just a smile* (page 37) and *Facetalking* (page 36.)

Blank the speech bubbles in a cartoon story including some three to six pictures. Ask students to form pairs, give a copy to each pair, and ask them to fill in the spaces so that they make up a meaningful conversation that fits the drawings. Have students exchange and read each other's stories in small groups. You may follow with a discussion on what clues they used, how the clues in the character's facial expression or body language were connected to words communicated, and what similarities resulted in the stories.

Variation 1:
To save classroom time, you may give the first half of the task as homework.

Variation 2:
Instead of using a cartoon, you may play a video tape with the sound turned off. Select a very short piece showing dramatic action or distinct changes in the facial expression, body posture, position or gestures of the characters.

Once again, please
role-playing a communication problem

Level	elementary/intermediate/advanced
Main goals	communication strategies, comprehension strategies
Language focus	stress, intonation, pronunciation
Preparation	role cards

The activity is designed to introduce and practise the use of feedback in a conversation.

Ask students what they say if they cannot understand what someone else is saying in a conversation. (You may use *This is confusing. I'm very confused:* a jazz chant from Graham, 1986, p.71.) Together with the students collect a list of possible expressions, such as:

> *I'm sorry, I didn't understand. Could you repeat that please?*
> *Pardon? I beg your pardon. What did you say?*
> *What's that again?*
> *What do you mean? I don't understand.*
> *Could you say that again, please – more slowly?*
> *I didn't get that. You lost me there.*
> *Could you explain this to me?*
> *I'm lost. I'm sorry, I didn't catch that bit.*
> *I'm sorry, I didn't follow you.*

You may also collect phrases for the speaker who is not understood:

> *Could you help with my pronunciation, please?*
> *I'm sorry, what I want to say is:....*

With the expressions at hand, the students can practise usage in short dialogues. Names and numbers can be especially difficult to catch. So, you may ask students to pick some dates, numbers or names that are important to them (e.g. their birth date, their mother's maiden name, or the street where they live) and take turns in dictating these to each other, asking for repetition when necessary. Alternatively, you may let students choose their topic, and ask one of each pair to whisper as if they had a sore throat.

When the pairs finish, ask them in what sort of situations they can use these expressions. (For example, when talking on the phone, at railway stations or airports, or with people who speak too fast.) Another possible follow up is to discuss differences in style among the expressions they used. You may use *Out in the world* (page 26) as a lead-in to this activity. See also *Dialogue repair* (below) for more practice in communication strategies.

Say that again
rephrasing simple statements

Level	intermediate/advanced
Main goals	communication strategies, rephrasing
Language focus	oral fluency practice

The point here is to practise the strategy of rephrasing an idea in order to make it clearer for the audience.

Students work in pairs. Explain that the aim of the activity is to keep conversation going, but only one in each pair can really communicate: student A will try to tell something to student B which student B (who is, for example, wearing headphones and listening to music) cannot hear or understand well, so he/she will ask 'What?' – again and again. (See *Once again, please* (above) for some alternatives to saying 'What?'.) Each time, student A must try to answer with a new variation of the same message.

You may choose the topic yourself and use the activity to review vocabulary, or let the students decide what to talk about. Pairs switch roles when they have exhausted possible variations. Follow with a discussion on situations when they can use paraphrasing (such as solving a misunderstanding, or getting round a word they don't remember or don't exactly know how to use).

Dialogue repair
analysing communication breakdown

Level	elementary/intermediate/advanced
Main goals	communication strategies, empathy
Language focus	grammar review
Preparation	script of dialogue on blackboard/OHP/handouts

The activity helps students focus on the communicative features of speech as opposed to form.

You can either make up a simple dialogue, or write one based on a student's written story (see *Out in the world* on page 26), in which communication takes a wrong track or fails altogether, at several points. Act out the dialogue with a volunteer, and ask the others to listen and think about how the problems could be avoided or solved. To give structure to the activity, draw a chart on the blackboard (or give it on handouts) and then fill it in – something like this:

(S)he thought/felt	(S)he said	(S)he should have said
I wonder what his profession is.	– What are you doing?	What do you do for a living?
I don't like to be disturbed when I'm reading the papers.	– I read the news.	I am reading the newspaper.
Is he a radio announcer?	– On the radio?	Do you work for a radio station?
Why is she talking about the radio?	– No! I read this newspaper!	I am reading this newspaper.
He is looking a little irritated.	– Do you works for an agency?	Oh, I thought you were an announcer. Do you work for a news agency?
What a silly question! I wish she would let me finish my reading.	– No, I don't want to sell anything! I just want to read the news.	Perhaps we could chat a little when I've got to the end of the news section?
I must have asked the wrong question.	– Oh, I'm sorry.	Oh, I didn't mean to disturb you.

Go through the dialogue and ask students what to put in the first and third columns for each sentence and why. You may discuss what types of mistakes (grammar, intonation, pronunciation) may hinder understanding. If there is time, you may ask students to act out the repaired version in pairs.

Recipe
rewriting a recipe to emphasise time order

Level	intermediate/advanced
Main goal	comprehension strategies
Language focus	written fluency practice, link words, adverbs of time
Preparation	handouts with recipe

In this activity the aim is to focus on structure and to introduce a tool for organising texts.

Choose a recipe which does not give the tasks as they are sequenced in time, such as the one following:

Hungarian goulash

You will need some beef, onions, carrots, root of parsley, parsley, potatoes, caraway seed, salt, black pepper, paprika, and some oil. Lightly fry the finely chopped onions, add the paprika and stir so that it dissolves without burning. Put in the beef – cleaned and chopped into cubes and simmer together with the seasoning as if making a stew. Add the carrots and root of parsley sliced up. When half-cooked, add the potatoes, too (peeled and chopped into smallish cubes). Always be sure to fill the pot with enough water to cover the vegetables. You may use broth instead of water. Serve as a rich soup, with fresh parsley sprinkled on top.

© Cambridge University Press 2000

Give copies to pairs or small groups and ask students to rewrite the text, carefully sorting out the tasks and adding link words (*first, after, then, finally*) to show the chronological order clearly. You may discuss if the text benefited from the rewriting, taking the inexperienced cook's view, and also, what other tools there may be to organise a text (such as similarities-differences, advantages-disadvantages, cause and effect, etc.).

For more practice in dealing with structures, look at *Essay writing in pairs* (page 68), *Reading assignment* (page 74), and *Mapping* (below).

Mapping
finding structure in a text

Level	intermediate/advanced
Main goal	comprehension strategies
Language focus	link words, pronouns, reading practice
Preparation	written passage from textbook or on handouts
Notes	especially useful for adult learners in higher education, visually oriented and analytically minded learners

This activity introduces a tool for understanding texts, and provides practice in finding structure and summarising.

Select a longer passage appropriate for the students and identify the main idea of the text. Write a word or expression on the blackboard that captures the main idea. Give each student a handout, and ask them to read the passage carefully, so that they fully understand the underlying logic and ideas, and ask them to draw a 'map' of the text around the key word that you have put on the blackboard. The map should indicate the logical flow of the text and the organisation of information. If the task is unfamiliar, you may provide a sample map based on a passage you have previously worked on. The map is to help the reader understand the structure of the text, so different readers may draw different maps to the same text. For example, the introduction entitled *Raising awareness* on page 15 of this book could be mapped like this:

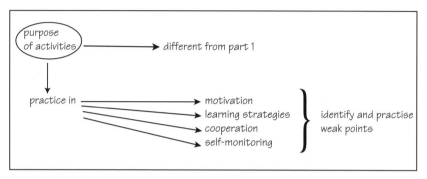

When the students have finished, have them compare the maps in small groups. (If possible, make sure that each group includes an analytically minded student.) If necessary, give groups specific questions to discuss, such as:

> *Did you use more or less the same words in your maps?*
> *If not, do you see the reason for the choice of words in the others' work?*
> *What creates cohesion between paragraphs in the text?*
> *Did you indicate this in your maps?*

Ask students to think about possible ways to structure a text. There are many such ways, e.g. following the chronological order of events, comparing options or objects, explaining the cause and then its effect, or listing advantages and disadvantages. If there is time, compile a list of such methods together with the whole class. As a homework assignment, you may ask each group to find examples for a different structure type, not necessarily written in the foreign language.

2.2.3 Community building

Making ends meet
combining sentence halves

Level	elementary/intermediate
Main goals	cooperation, creativity
Language focus	sentence structure, conditionals

This activity requires students to rethink their ideas and try to reshape them so that they match their partners'. It may also provide useful practice in conditionals.

Divide the class into two equal groups. Write a conditional sentence on the blackboard, marking the '*if* clause' and the 'result clause'. Then, ask students to work on their own and write three to five half sentences, students in one group writing *if* clauses, those in the other group writing result clauses. When they have finished, ask them to find a partner from the other group, look at the sentence halves they have, and try to put together meaningful sentences. They can make any necessary changes and create some amusing or unusual combinations, as long as they can explain the situation they had in mind (see the examples below). You may follow with a whole class discussion on the criteria (of grammar and meaning) of matching sentence halves.

If I have time . . .	*. . . I'll buy a new car.*
If you read this letter . . .	*. . . he will go to work.*
If you wash my car . . .	*. . . he watches TV.*

If you wash the car, you can watch TV after supper. (older brother to his little sister)
If you read this letter, you can buy a new car. (chain letter about making money)
If I have the time, I'll go to work. (irritated son, in response to mother's scolding)

Variation:
You may apply this activity to any other grammatical pattern that includes two distinct parts of a sentence, such as the simple past-past continuous contrast or sentences with temporal clauses.

Co-authors
writing a 50 word story in pairs

Level	elementary/intermediate/advanced
Main goals	cooperation, personalising input
Language focus	vocabulary review, written fluency practice, patterns of reduction

This activity challenges students to work together in a rather tight structure. To get them to think consciously about the various aspects of cooperation, you may do *Two in the bush* first (a simpler version of this activity on page 39).

To give students an idea of what you mean by simple stories, you may read an example story (see in the Appendix) before doing the exercise. Ask students to pick four to six useful or important words from the previous lesson's vocabulary or a text they have just worked on. Then ask them to get into pairs, combine the two sets of words they have and write a 50 word story using all these words, or as many as they can. After ten to fifteen minutes, ask if any of the pairs have their story finished, and have them read it to the class.

You may follow with a discussion on how pairs worked together: how they divided tasks, how they made decisions, if there was a dominant person in the pair, etc. (See the questions for *Two in the bush* on page 40.) Alternatively, you can work on the examples of how they reduced structures to meet the 50 word limit.

Essay writing in pairs
writing a draft and an introduction

Level	intermediate/advanced
Main goals	cooperation, peer evaluation
Language focus	written fluency practice, writing a draft
Note	especially useful for adult learners in higher education

This activity challenges students to express ideas very clearly in a draft and in an introduction, and it gives them immediate feedback on how well they can do this. You may need to give them some practice in organising ideas before this activity, e.g. *Recipe* (page 64) or *Mapping* (page 65).

Give students an essay title and ask them to sketch a draft for an essay. Have pairs exchange drafts and write the introduction for each other's essay. When they have finished, they read each other's writing and discuss if they understood the ideas contained in the draft, and whether the introduction suited the draft. You may follow with a whole class discussion on the respective functions of an introduction and a draft. You may also discuss the difficulties of getting one's ideas across, the misunderstandings that may crop up, and ways of dealing with these.

(In English-speaking cultures, the purpose of an introduction is to outline the contents of the main text. In other cultures, the introduction may be more general, or it may only serve to raise the readers' interest.)

Check your facts
role-playing a job interview

Level	intermediate/advanced
Main goals	cooperation, sharing personal experiences
Language focus	interviewing, intonation, contradicting politely, tag questions
Preparation	handouts with exercise on tag questions

The set-up of this activity requires students to contradict each other in polite ways, which is an important part of the ability to cooperate.

Explain to students that they are going to role-play a job interview: this is to make clear the need for being polite. Explain the details of the procedure, and, if necessary, provide some useful phrases, such as: *Not really . . . , I wouldn't say that was the case . . . , Actually, no . . . , Well, not exactly . . .*, etc. To prepare for the interview, students write down three true and three false statements about themselves on a slip of paper.

Then they interview each other in pairs: the one to be interviewed passes his or her statements to the interviewer, who will check the accuracy of these. The interviewer should assume the information is accurate and should use either falling tag questions or statements with falling intonation. When the interviewer hits upon an untruth, the interviewee must set him or her right, but in a very polite way.

In the next round, students switch roles. You may follow with a discussion on why politeness is important in this situation, and how it can be important in others. (Adapted from Kenworthy, 1987.)

Variation 1:
You may ask students beforehand to prepare a curriculum vitae mixing accurate and false information for homework, and then use this in the lesson.

Variation 2:
You may skip the CV writing or information giving phase and ask students to guess facts about their partners and express these as statements when doing the interview.

Tea or coffee?
discussing tastes

Level	elementary/intermediate
Main goals	group cohesion, sharing personal experiences
Language focus	expressing feelings and preferences, simple present, *like* + gerund

From time to time it is useful to cut across cliques in the class and give learners a chance to work and exchange ideas with new people. The following activity provides one example of how to do this.
Draw a matrix on the blackboard like this:

I prefer	coffee	tea
beer		
wine		

You may substitute potato or rice for the alcoholic drinks, or any other matter of choice (e.g. cats or dogs, summer or winter) that is likely to divide the class into distinct groups. Ask students to place themselves in the matrix, then assign each cell to a corner of the classroom, and ask them to go to the corner that fits their tastes best. So, if someone prefers tea to coffee, and wine to beer (as Anita does), she should be in the bottom right corner.

If none of the groups that form contains more than eight students, simply ask them to explore their tastes in detail: how often they have their favourite drink, with how much sugar, any milk, dry or sweet wine, etc. With beginners, ask them to collect other things that they all like.

If the groups are too large, ask them to split according to some further aspect of their tastes (such as taking sugar or not, liking dry wine or not) and then continue as above. Alternatively, splitting may become a task itself, if you ask them to find something that divides them into two or three more or less equal subgroups. Try to use these groups in a subsequent activity.

Note 1:
The advantage of the matrix set-up is that the division between groups cannot get very sharp, since each group shares one preference with one other group. This reduces the risk of unpleasant feelings of isolation or exclusion.

Note 2:
You may use this activity to practise the recognition of categories, a useful strategy in learning. Ask the groups to make a list of other things (not only food) that they all like. When they have ten to fifteen items, ask them to arrange these into categories. Discuss if they had a strategy in collecting the items, and how they could use categories in their learning.

Variation:
Brandes and Ginnis (1992) suggest a similar matrix activity as a lead-in to discussions. First you draw an imaginary line, show its two ends which

represent extremes of opinion, e.g. *I hate/love politics*, and ask the students to move their chairs to the point that would correspond to their attitudes. Then you can introduce another, related question, draw an imaginary line across the first one, and ask learners to find their position in this second dimension as well. Now you have four quarters ready to discuss their opinions. (The second dimension is really optional: in fact, the more complicated the issue, the better it is to have only one.)

What do we have in common?
discussing common tastes, interests, etc.

Level	elementary/intermediate/advanced
Main goals	sharing ideas, group cohesion
Language focus	expressing feelings and preferences
Preparation	result of student questionnaires

This activity gives you a chance to show students that you listen to them when they tell you about themselves. As it takes some willingness to give up existing cliques in the class, it may be necessary to use some other community building activities to prepare students for this one.

Once you have collected some information from the students, use this data to group them, putting together the ones who share some characteristics (e.g. if they wrote about their interests, form one group for sports fans, one for music addicts, etc.). In class, announce that you are going to play a game. Pick someone from each group that most of the others would be willing to accept as a leader, give him/her the list of names for the particular group, and ask him/her to gather the group as quickly as possible.

The next task is to find out what they all have in common. Give only the general topic (e.g. interests and hobbies). It will be the leader's role to direct the discussion. If some groups finish too early, ask them to explore the different origins of or reasons for the interest they share, or to find other common characteristics of the group. For a further option see the second note for *Tea or coffee?* (page 70).

Working as a group
discussing roles in group work

Level	elementary/intermediate/advanced
Main goals	group cohesion, cooperation
Language focus	arguing, persuading
Preparation	handouts (or OHP) with interaction patterns
Note	suits adult learners especially

The point here is to have students think about how they can contribute to group work. It is important to note, however, that a single activity cannot make old routines change. You may find it useful to do *Group work analysis* (page 40) before doing this exercise.

After some activity involving loosely structured group work, give each group a handout with several interaction patterns, such as:

Based on: T. Wright: Roles of Teachers and Learners, pp.38-39.

Ask them to choose the pattern that best characterises their work as a group, and write their names into the chart. (Or copy it from the OHP with their names.)

When they finish, ask the class as a whole to think about the meaning of the charts: what sorts of roles go with certain positions and what sorts of interactions take place. Make a list of these on the blackboard. Roles may include: secretary, devil's advocate, discussion leader, judge, idea-person, yes-man, analyser, etc.

Next, ask students to work in groups again and consider which interaction patterns and which roles are most efficient regarding, firstly, the accomplishment of the task, and secondly, the maximum involvement and practice for all group members. Ask them which requirement is more important for them, and on that basis prepare a list of important roles and rules for interaction. (Rules may include: giving everyone a chance to speak, being polite, accepting majority opinion, tolerating differences of opinion, etc.)

You could then use the students' suggestions to prepare role cards for a group discussion activity. Alternatively, you may have the students do that: explain that you will have a discussion in the following lesson and give them blank cards to fill in.

Variation:
You may use the same interaction patterns to start a discussion on the general organisation of group work: did participants work closely together, was group leadership democratic, laissez-faire, or authoritarian,

was their work strictly or loosely organised, did everybody participate equally, etc.

Making rain
inventing a group ritual

Level	intermediate/advanced
Main goals	group cohesion, creativity
Language focus	oral fluency practice

The activity draws on the idea that one of the cohesive forces in a community is the common practice of rituals.

Ask learners to think of examples of rituals and discuss what functions they may serve, such as 'making' rain to help the growth of crops, or welcoming new members into a community. Rituals may be based on very simple things, like greeting each other in the morning. For example, Ágota remembers that boys in her primary school class would sit in a row along the long bench in the main lobby each morning, and when a classmate arrived, he would shake hands one by one with all those already there. For some reason, girls had no such ritual.

Ask students to get into groups and choose a similar function relevant for the whole group (e.g. passing a difficult exam, having nice weather at the weekend, celebrating success), and invent a ritual for the group to practise. Allow time for groups to present their rituals to the whole class. You may schedule presentations over several lessons.

2.2.4 Self-monitoring

Watch your slips
correcting mistakes in written work

Main goals	identifying difficulties, self-correction
Note	works best as a homework assignment

This activity invites students to work on their mistakes in writing. You need to explain that this task helps them take control over their learning – lest some of them may feel abandoned or frustrated, thinking that you are trying to save time at their expense.

When marking some written work of the students, do not give the correct version: only indicate if the mistake is that of spelling (sp), grammar (g), word order (wo), or perhaps style (s), in the case of advanced learners. Ask students to correct the mistakes for the next lesson and write a note for you on those they could not correct. You may answer these questions individually, writing a note to each student or, if problems overlap, you may deal with them by having a remedy session for the whole class.

Speak to yourself
recording and analysing a short talk

Level	elementary/intermediate/advanced
Main goals	identifying difficulties, self-evaluation
Language focus	oral fluency practice
Preparation	evaluation sheets
Note	works best as a homework assignment

This activity invites students to identify fluency, pronunciation or other problems in their speech. You may need to explain to students that the task is solely for their benefit and you will not use it for evaluation purposes. (*Doing* the task may still be a condition of getting a good mark.)

Ask students to choose a topic that they find interesting and/or easy to talk about, do a one to three minute talk on the topic, and record it. Remind them *not to read* their speech! Give each student an evaluation sheet, which they should fill in while listening to their own talk. (See an example opposite.) You may spread this assignment over one semester and check the work of two or three students each week. Comment on the talk and on the self-evaluation of each student (be as reassuring as possible) and discuss in class possible exercises that may help them improve.

Reading assignment
monitoring the use of reading strategies

Level	intermediate/advanced
Main goals	identifying difficulties, self-evaluation, reading strategies
Language focus	reading practice
Preparation	work sheets for reading
Note	works best as a homework assignment

You may need to prepare your students for this task with some activities on reading skills, such as *Weather forecast* (page 33) and *How to read* (page 35). Also, you may need to reassure students that the task is solely for their benefit and you will not use it for evaluation purposes.

Evaluation sheet for short talk

Speaking skills

yes/no How could you improve on this skill?

1 Fluency

Did you often stop and hesitate   before starting a new sentence?

before starting a difficult word?

searching for a suitable word?

2 Grammatical accuracy

Did you make any mistakes that you never do in writing?

Did you make the same mistake several times? What was this?

. . . .

3 Pronunciation

On the whole did you find your pronunciation natural?

Did you notice any slips (when you mispronounce something you normally know)?

Did you have a general problem with particular sounds? Which ones?

. . . .

4 Stress and intonation

On the whole did you find your stress and intonation natural?

Did you notice any problems with a particular sentence type or intonation pattern? Or any words with the wrong stress?

. . . .

5 Structure

Did you find your talk logically structured?

Was it easy to follow?

© Cambridge University Press 2000

The students must be aware of some reading skills such as skimming, or guessing from context. Ask students to choose a text appropriate to their level and interest (can be a newspaper article, an anecdote from a story collection, or a simplified story from an easy reading series – you may need to help them find a suitable one) and give each a work sheet to fill in while they are reading. See the example on the next page.

You may spread this assignment over one semester and check the work of two or three students each week. Comment on the self-evaluation of each student (be as reassuring as possible) and suggest some exercises that may help them improve.

Evaluation sheet for reading assignment

Read the text twice. The first time read it quickly to identify the subject and the main idea, and to see the structure of the paragraphs. The second time, read carefully to understand all the details. Take your time to try and guess unfamiliar words from the context. Do not use a dictionary!

I began the first reading at ☐☐ ☐☐

I finished the first reading at ☐☐ ☐☐

After the first reading:

    the subject of the passage is . . . .

    the main idea is . . . .

    I understood all the details in all the paragraphs . . . . %

    I could guess all new words from the context . . . . %

I began the second reading at ☐☐ ☐☐

I finished the second reading at ☐☐ ☐☐

After the second reading:

    the subject of the passage is . . . .

    the main idea is . . . .

    I understood all the details in all the paragraphs . . . . %

    I could guess all new words from the context . . . .%

Based on the above notes:

	yes/ no	How could you improve on this skill?
Did you read quicker the first time than the second?		
Could you focus on general understanding in your first reading?		
Did you stop to figure out new words in your first reading? (hopefully not!)		
In the second reading, could you guess most new words from the context?		
Could you understand each paragraph even if there were some new words?		
On the whole did you find the task difficult?		

What's the point?
reviewing the aims of classroom tasks

Level	elementary/intermediate/advanced
Main goal	focusing on the learning process
Preparation	list of activities on handouts or OHP

The point in this activity is to have students consciously think about what aims there may be in their learning and how they can achieve these aims.

After a few weeks of teaching, give students a list of activities you used with the class, and a list of aims or purposes these were supposed to serve, as in: 'role-playing a visit to the dentist' or 'practising new vocabulary'. Explain that the two lists are in mixed order, and ask students to match each activity with its purpose(s). When they have finished, check on some of the less obvious activities and ask if there were any that students were hesitant about. It may be useful feedback for you to collect and read through all answers.

Variation:
You may ask students for additional feedback on each activity: if it succeeded in its aim, if it achieved an aim other than what was intended, what could have made it more effective, etc.

Your resources
discussing how to learn outside the classroom

Main goals	focusing on the learning process, creativity, sharing ideas
Language focus	*can/may/might*

The aim of the activity is to share ideas on how or where to learn the foreign language outside the classroom.

For homework, ask your students to think about things they can use as a resource for learning the foreign language (some conventional ones would be foreign language books, newspapers, or subtitled films) and an explanation of how to use them. In class, pool the ideas, either writing a list on the blackboard for the whole class, or in groups of around ten students. You may need to supply some less obvious examples (such as reading product labels) to get them started. After the discussion, ask the class/groups if they have heard anything new or interesting which they might really use as a resource. Encourage them to use *can / may / might* to express shades of possibility. You may ask them to copy the list for themselves arranging the ideas in order of usefulness (or rather, the likelihood that they would use them). See *Notice board* (page 81) for a further development of this activity.

Further reading

Baudains, Richard and Baudains, Marjorie (1989) *Alternatives*, Longman offer a good range of learner centred activities to keep up motivation.

Burbridge, Nicky, Gray, Peta, Levy, Sheila, and Rinvolucri, Mario (1996) *Letters*, Oxford University Press suggests some good ideas to increase interaction between students in and outside the classroom, some adaptable to email.

Davis, Paul and Rinvolucri, Mario (1990) *The Confidence Book*, Longman includes a good selection of activities to boost learners' confidence.

Deller, Sheelagh (1990) *Lessons from the Learner, Student-Generated Activities for the Language Classroom*, Longman helps teachers to involve learners in producing materials for the classroom.

Gerngross, Günter and Puchta, Herbert (1992) *Creative Grammar Practice: Getting Learners to Use Both Sides of the Brain*, Longman includes complete lessons and activities to practise difficult grammar structures in non-analytical, creative ways.

Gerngross, Günter and Puchta, Herbert (1992) *Pictures in Action*, Prentice Hall includes a range of activities for creative writing and sharing information.

Graham, Caroline (1986) *Small Talk: More Jazz Chants*, Oxford University Press is a collection of chants in jazz rhythms to teach intonation, stress, and everyday expressions in American English.

Hadfield, Jill (1992) *Classroom Dynamics*, Oxford University Press offers some empathy activities, and some to ensure participation.

Kenworthy, Joanne (1987) *Teaching English Pronunciation*, Longman includes some excellent listening activities for the development of learning strategies.

Kreidler, William J. (1984) *Creative Conflict Resolution: More Than 200 Activities for Keeping Peace in the Classroom*, Scott, Foresman and Co. may help teachers respond creatively and constructively to classroom conflicts. Also includes some activities on cooperation.

Lawlor, Michael (1988) *Inner Track Learning*, Pilgrims describes techniques to bring right brain hemisphere faculties into the learning process: some may be useful for teaching learning strategies.

Lindstromberg, Seth (ed.) (1990) *The Recipe Book*, Longman offers a good range of learner centred activities to keep up motivation.

Littlejohn, Anna and Hicks, Diana (1996) *Cambridge English for Schools*, Cambridge University Press is a course book designed to promote learner choice and decision making. It includes activities drawing on learners' knowledge in other subject areas and on the world around.

Moskowitz, Gertrude (1987) *Caring and Sharing in the Foreign Language Classroom: A Sourcebook on Humanistic Techniques*, Newbury House Publishers is a collection of activities to build motivation and increase learner involvement.

O'Malley, J. Michael and Chamot, Anna Uhl (1990) *Learning Strategies in Second Language Acquisition*, Cambridge University Press offers some ideas on how to teach strategies in language learning.

Puchta, Herbert and Schratz, Michael (1993) *Teaching Teenagers, Model Activity Sequences for Humanistic Language Learning*, Longman includes some excellent activities to develop empathy and cooperation. Also reports on a case study of dealing with a class used to traditional teaching methods.

Reid, Joy M. (1995) *Learning Styles in the English as a Second Language Classroom*, Heinle and Heinle offers some practical ideas on how to accommodate teaching to particular learning styles. The chapters on visual, auditory and kinaesthetic learners may be especially useful for teaching learning strategies.

Strange, Derek and Collie, Joanne (1996) *Double Take*, Oxford University Press includes activities for learner strategies training, designed to interest teenagers.

Ur, Penny and Wright, Andrew (1992) *Five-Minute Activities*, Cambridge University Press offers a good range of learner centred activities to keep up motivation.

Willing, Ken (1989) *Teaching How to Learn, Learning Strategies in ESL*, National Centre for English Language Teaching and Research, Sydney, Macquarie University includes a discussion of learning styles and strategies, and some activities.

2.3 Transferring roles

The activities in this section are all examples of involving students in the various tasks that come up in any teaching-learning situation. Most examples entail handing over roles that are traditionally held by the teacher.

There are two main reasons why we think this useful and necessary. For one, learners can only assume responsibility for their learning if they have some control over the learning process. For another, increasing independence may evoke and reinforce responsible and autonomous attitudes. This of course only happens if students are ready to accept the challenge of independence, and this is exactly why we devised a step-by-step process of responsibility development.

In this section we have grouped activities according to the nature of the tasks handed over to the learner, moving gradually towards tasks that require a high degree of independence. In the heading of each activity, we have indicated the particular task passed on to the learners. So, we start from handling devices in the classroom, then present examples of learners preparing or choosing learning materials, of learners being a source of information, of peer monitoring and correction, and of learners presenting a model of the target language. Next we include examples of how to involve students in decisions about the learning process. At the end of the section we describe the procedure of negotiating rules of behaviour in the classroom in the framework of a class contract.

We are by no means proposing that you must take your learners through all these stages. The scope and nature of learner involvement should correspond to the capabilities of your students and to your views on teaching. You may find it useful at this point to go to the list of roles and tasks in the classroom (page 101) and consider which of these you would be happy to give over to your students. We invite you however to experiment with stretching the limits of your views. If you asked your students to do the responsibility questionnaire (page 19) at the beginning of the development process, you may have them do that again, and discuss the changes in their attitudes.

Besides increasing learner involvement, most activities in the section serve objectives concerning learning strategies, motivation, self-monitoring, and community building, and focus on some language point as well.

Take one and pass it on
allocating small tasks in the classroom

Main goals   helping in classroom arrangements, group cohesion
Language focus   responding to polite requests

There are a number of small tasks or technical arrangements in the lesson that you can ask the students to do. Getting them involved encourages autonomy, it may increase group cohesion (as they are doing things for the benefit of the whole group), and sometimes also save some time for you. An extra benefit is that you can use the target language in a natural situation.

The point here is to hand over tasks that carry a certain degree of responsibility: you entrust your students to do something that would normally be done by you. Asking learners to open the window or draw the curtains will not do much in the way of increasing autonomy.

You can ask students to hand out materials ('take one and pass it on'), to arrange desks before and after the lesson, to check attendance, or to handle the OHP. If some of these tasks occur regularly, you may discuss and establish a routine of taking turns in administering them.

Variation:
Some technical tasks require a little bit more than technical skills, but may nevertheless be passed on to students. For example, if you use background music as stimulation for a free writing activity, you can ask one of the students to stop the recorder when he or she considers it appropriate. This of course involves not only pressing a button but also making a decision on when the activity should be stopped, thus inviting the student to monitor the activity of others, and giving him/her a chance to control the time allotted to the activity.

Notice board
sharing ideas about learning outside the classroom

Level   intermediate/advanced
Main goals   being a source of information, bringing in outside knowledge, sharing ideas
Language focus   writing brief, neat notices and patterns of reduction

This activity encourages students to share all the information that may help their learning of the foreign language outside the classroom. This may be especially useful for the students who trust the suggestions of their peers more than those coming from the teacher.

At the beginning of a lesson, ask students if they are planning to do or have done anything during the week that has some language learning value. Do this a couple of times. If you find that there is enough interest and that there are enough activities going on, ask students if they would like to share such news regularly. If their response is positive, discuss how they would like to share their news with the others. One way to do this is to set aside five minutes of class time each week for reading announcements. Another way is for them to write their news in the form of short notices that they put on a notice board for everyone to read (perhaps during the break). The announcements may not concern events only, but may include good books to read, or sources of foreign language related materials, such as a second-hand music shop, or a café that provides foreign language newspapers.

Once a routine is established, you can help maintain attention by regularly referring to notices, including them in classroom activities whenever possible, and asking for feedback on who used them and with what success.

Variation:
You may encourage students to use the notice board to display ideas/plans etc. not specifically related to language learning, but written in the target language.

Message in a bottle
sending a message via the Internet or post

Level	intermediate/advanced
Main goals	choosing learning material, bringing in outside knowledge
Language focus	writing a message
Note	see below for a variation that does not require any technical equipment

This activity invites the students to use their knowledge of the foreign language outside the classroom and find out something of interest to them. The activity also serves as a side-track from the dominant route of information between teacher and learner: this helps to weaken the students' reliance on the teacher.

Brainstorm about the use of the Internet: the function of contacting people is almost certain to come up. Explain to students that you would like them to use this function and contact someone else in another country and exchange messages. A lot of web pages (e.g. run by universities, large international companies, or public institutions) invite the browser to contact the owner of the page. Students can ask for some information, join a discussion group, or write to a personal home page: it is all their choice. Ask them to report on their findings to the whole class or in groups.

Variation:
Most international companies run a help line or provide an address for queries: you may ask students to write a letter of complaint/enquiry/ congratulations about some product they have bought or service they have used, and send it to the company.

Sharing knowledge
helping each other to understand a text

Level	intermediate/advanced
Main goals	choosing learning materials, being a source of information, cooperation
Language focus	question forms
Preparation	text for reading activity
Note	may take up half or all of the lesson

This activity makes students turn to each other for information rather than to the teacher. This will develop their ability to cope with a task using limited resources and will lessen their dependence on the teacher.

After a reading comprehension task, give each student slips of paper and ask them to write down a question for everything (or the most important things) that they cannot understand in the text. This may include the meaning or use of certain words, or of a whole paragraph, as long as the questions are not too vague. Then ask them to get into groups, collect their questions, and exchange them with another group. Students in the other group will try and answer (and return to the sender) as many of the questions as they can, within a set time limit. They may do this individually, allocating the questions in some way, or they may choose to cooperate. You can pool and assign the remaining questions for homework, or collect the slips and answer them in the next lesson.

Retranslating
translating a group mate's translation

Level	intermediate/advanced
Main goals	producing learning materials, self-evaluation
Language focus	translating
Preparation	handouts
Note	only works in a monolingual class

This activity is designed so that students can immediately correct and evaluate their performance without having to rely on the teacher, and also to help them develop their own insights into correspondences or lack of correspondences between the target and native languages.

Select two short passages (A and B) that do not contain new vocabulary, or very little. Prepare students for the text with some lead-in questions (e.g. select interviews with famous people and have students guess the names before giving them the texts). Divide the class into two groups of equal number, and give copies of passage A to one half and passage B to the other half. Make sure that students see only the text they are working on. Ask students to start translating the text into their mother tongue.

After five to ten minutes stop students and ask them to exchange their translations with someone in the other group. Now, they have to translate the text (the translation written by their peer) back to the foreign language. After another five to ten minutes students may look at the original versions. Have pairs who exchanged translations sit together and discuss their work: how and why the passages changed in the course of translations. It may be helpful to put a few types of differences on the blackboard, such as choice of words, use of adjectives, verb tense, active-passive voice, etc.

The brochure collection
simplifying instructions about using a device

Level	intermediate/advanced
Main goals	producing learning materials, bringing in outside knowledge, communication strategies
Language focus	written fluency practice, giving instructions, imperatives

You may encourage student involvement and motivation by asking them to produce materials for the whole class to use. This activity is one example of how to do this.

Ask students to find a brochure written in the target language that explains the use of some domestic device (kitchenware, DIY or music equipment), ideally something they use themselves. They can also work from a brochure written in several languages including the target language.

Ask them to read the instructions of usage at home, simplify the technical wording of the original text, and make it easy to understand. They should write this simple version omitting direct references to the name of the device. In class, each student explains the use of the equipment to the other members of the group (or whole class if there are less than seven students) who will try to guess the device. You can round off the activity with a collection of useful technical terms or pairs of formal and informal words expressing the same meaning.

Party
role-playing party conversation

Level	elementary/intermediate/advanced
Main goals	producing learning materials, creativity, sharing personal experiences
Language focus	greeting people, asking for and giving personal information

Role plays already give considerable freedom to the students in the choice of the language they use. This activity is an example of further increasing this freedom by inviting students to write their own role cards.

Tell students that you will give a mini party for the class. (Bring some snacks or refreshments if you can.) The speciality of the party is that participants can choose their personality. Just as in a fancy dress ball, they can be someone else or borrow some characteristics they would like to have. The first time you may give a list of characteristics (age, gender, nationality, place of residence, profession, family, hobbies), and ask students to think up a personality they want to represent. Give them about five minutes to write their role cards. If necessary, prepare them for the party phase: ask them about ways to approach somebody, to introduce oneself, to start a conversation, etc., and put some useful phrases on the blackboard. Then the party begins: students walk around and talk to others, with the aim of discovering each other's personalities.

Variation 1:
Once students are familiar with the activity, you may leave the number and type of personal characteristics completely open.

Variation 2:
You may apply some interesting restriction, such as, all professions should be in some way connected to music, everybody should do some sport, everybody should be happy with life (for different reasons), etc. If students like the idea, you may also let them decide on restrictions or themes: from time to time volunteers can come up with suggestions and organise a mini party for the class.

Variation 3:
You may use the well-known 'Find someone who . . .', to give more structure to conversations during the party. When students have written

their role cards, ask them to write down what kind of people they are hoping to meet at the party. Encourage them to ask more detailed questions to the people who fulfilled their hopes.

Student talks
giving a talk to the class

Level	intermediate/advanced
Main goals	producing learning materials, being a source of information, bringing in outside knowledge
Language focus	oral fluency practice, listening to peers
Preparation	handouts with task sheet

The message of this activity for the students is that their contributions are an important part of the lesson and of learning in general, and that learning can take place in student-student interaction as well.

When students have had some experience in speaking freely on a set topic (see for example *Speak to yourself* on page 74), introduce the idea of talks. You may give one yourself, so that students can see what exactly is expected of them. Starting with the more able students, ask them to choose a topic, and prepare a short (five to ten minute) talk. Remind students that you would like the talk to be based on spontaneous speech, not a read-aloud essay. You may offer to help them find out about the topic and give them materials in the target language.

If you fear that some students tend to pay attention only to you, and not their peers, you may ask the presenters to prepare a task sheet that includes specific questions based on the information in the talk. They may hand out copies of this for the class to fill in while listening to the talk.

Assign a couple of talks to be presented for each lesson. In a large class, talks may run simultaneously in small groups. Encourage students to ask the presenter some questions after the talk, and discuss what and why they did not understand. You may try to let the presenter lead the discussion, and help only when necessary.

Variation 1:
Talks may be organised in several forms, and some students may prefer one over the other. It may help ease inhibitions if you allow students to choose the form they like: such as standing in front of the class or sitting among them in a circle, or doing the talk together with a friend.

Variation 2:
You may prepare a task sheet with questions on the difficulties listeners encounter (see *Tuning in* on page 31), or general ones about the structure

and quality of the presentation, or a combination of the two, depending on the listening strategy you want students to practise.

The neighbourhood project
collecting information on the neighbourhood

Level	intermediate/advanced
Main goals	producing learning materials, being a source of information, cooperation, bringing in outside knowledge
Language focus	integrated skills
Note	takes up considerable time and may spread over several lessons

Projects can be a good way to develop responsible attitudes. In a good project the task is appropriate to the level and abilities of the students, and it is very clearly stated. Other than that, groups are given as much freedom as possible in deciding how to achieve their aim. We provide one example below, and some further suggestions for topics under Variation 1.

Ask students what facilities they would check out first if they moved into another neighbourhood. Pool all ideas, and then explain that you would like them to prepare a presentation on their own neighbourhood, which would contain all the appealing features of the area. They can include personal features, such as a friendly assistant in the video shop, and more standard ones, such as good public transport. Ask them to form groups on the basis of where they live – students who would be left alone can either decide to do the project on their own or join a group of their choice. Depending on available facilities in the school, you can ask students to take photos, prepare a video clip, make interviews, etc. You may set aside some classroom time for project work but some of the work will inevitably require out of class meetings. You may compensate for this by setting a relatively comfortable deadline – it is best if you discuss this with the students and agree on something that suits all of you. Agree on the possible forms of presentation as well, such as a poster, a talk illustrated with slides, a video taped guided tour, or a brochure (in several copies).

Have one presentation in each lesson, and if possible place it at the beginning of the lesson. Ask students to take notes on the features they found most attractive. When the class has seen all the presentations, respond in a positive way to both the form (language use, cooperation, etc.) and the contents of the performance of each group. You may encourage students to invite other groups to their neighbourhood and, if you have the time, you may visit one recommended place in each area

87

yourself! Discuss favourite features with the class. If you want to mark or otherwise evaluate the performance of the groups, you may ask them to write a diary of how they worked together on the project.

Variation 1:
In further projects the students may collect information about foreign countries, seek out and interview speakers of the target language living in their country, produce a newspaper, write an illustrated diary, or organise an advertising campaign for a favourite music group/film/dish etc. (See also Haines 1987, and Ribé and Vidal 1993.)

Variation 2:
You may ask students to check out a feature that they liked in the presentation of another group (e.g. go to a recommended café or shop) and write a report to you on the experience.

Variation 3:
As a follow-up activity you may ask the students to prepare a general brochure that includes all the areas. In a small class, you may do this together, pooling important features on the blackboard. You may also make it another project: ask students to form new groups, so that in each group they have representatives of all the neighbourhoods and produce a brochure together. They cannot include all the information they had in their earlier presentations, so they have to agree on what the best features were.

All you have always wanted to know . . .
asking questions about a famous person

Level	elementary/intermediate/advanced
Main goals	producing learning materials, being a source of information, bringing in outside knowledge
Language focus	simple past, asking questions (scanning or focused listening)
Preparation	(written or recorded passage on the life of a famous person)
Note	you may use this activity to introduce a new topic

The point of this activity is that students ask and answer each other, and not the teacher, about a topic they are genuinely interested to learn about.

Ask students about famous people whose lives have aroused their curiosity. Using their suggestions, make a list of names on the blackboard and get the class to agree on one or two people that they all find interesting. For homework, ask them to put down some of the information they have about one of these people, and some questions on things they would like to know about this person. You may suggest that students search for more information in magazines, books, or on the Internet.

In the next lesson, have each student read his or her notes to the class (or in smaller groups if the class is too large) while the others listen carefully to find out if any of their questions are answered. Provided that you have a suitable passage, you may read it or play the recording at this point, and then ask students how many of their questions still remained unanswered. If there is someone in the class who knows a lot about the particular celebrity, invite the others to put some of their questions to him/her.

Variation 1:
You can use the same framework to explore other topics, such as exotic countries and animals, scientific inventions, bygone civilisations, or one that the students choose for themselves.

Variation 2:
As an alternative follow up, you may ask the students to pick one of their questions that does not seem too difficult to answer, and write that on a slip of paper, with their names. Students exchange slips, and search for the answer as homework. This variation encourages students to rely on each other rather than on the teacher.

Writing a quiz
groups write questions about a famous person

Level	elementary/intermediate/advanced
Main goals	producing learning materials, being a source of knowledge, bringing in outside knowledge
Language focus	giving information, giving instructions, summarising, question forms
Note	works best as a homework assignment

The activity gives students an opportunity to work on a topic of interest to them, and to share their knowledge with their group. We provide one example below, and ideas for other topics in Variation 1.

Towards the end of a lesson, ask students about the celebrities that they like, and make up a list of names on the blackboard. Then ask them to form groups (or pairs, in a small class) and write a quiz on the life and habits of a famous person (not necessarily from the list) as homework. Allow them a few days or one week to collect information and produce a sheet of five to ten questions that you may copy for the whole class to fill in, and a separate answer sheet which they keep. They should leave enough space on the sheet for short answers. Ask them to give a name to their group and put this on the task sheet, and keep their work a secret. When all the groups have turned in their quizzes, organise a quiz session in the next lesson (see below).

Variation 1:
Other quiz topics may include: historical events, traditions, the origin of national holidays, sports, films, or any other topic of the students' choice. See also Variation 1 for *All you have always wanted to know . . .* (page 88).

Variation 2:
You may do this activity in several classes in the school and then do the quiz session across classes.

Quiz session
groups solve and evaluate answers to quiz questons

Level	elementary/intermediate/advanced
Main goals	peer evaluation, bringing in outside knowledge, cooperation
Language focus	giving short answers
Preparation	copies of student-made quizzes or tests

Evaluation is usually assumed to be the teacher's task. This activity invites students to set the norm and evaluate each other's performance against it. Some students may feel uncomfortable about this: making evaluation mutual and having students work in groups reduces this risk.

For this activity you need a quiz (or just a list of questions, such as a comprehension test or some other language exercise) written by pairs or groups of students, either in the previous lesson or as a homework assignment. Make copies of each list or quiz, enough for all the groups or pairs in the class.

Then organise the quiz session as follows: students work in the same pairs or groups as when they wrote the quiz. Give each group one quiz, other than their own, and when any of the groups have finished with the questions, give them another one, until the end of the time (ten to fifteen minutes) set for this phase. While students are working, sort out the completed quizzes according to their authors. Then give each completed sheet to the group who wrote the quiz, and ask them to check answers, announce the group who had the most correct answers, and return the answer sheets to the groups who wrote the answers. Allow some time for students to look at the correct answers and ask any questions.

Variation:
You may ask groups to mark completed sheets for both grammar and content.

Token game
tracking involvment in a group discussion

Level   intermediate/advanced
Main goals   calling on peers, self-monitoring, group cohesion
Language focus   oral fluency practice (*should/could have*, modals)
Preparation   matches or other tokens (bits of paper, paper clips, etc.)

In this activity students are invited to manage a discussion. The activity makes them think about how and why they take part in group work.

Before starting a group discussion, give each learner the same number of tokens (depending on the size of the group and the time available), e.g. matches. Arrange chairs in a circle, and place a chair, or a hat, or some other suitable object in the middle. Explain that students should put one token into the hat whenever they want to say or ask something. Alternatively, you may put all the tokens in the middle and ask students to pick one when they wish to speak: this saves you some time setting up the activity, and does not limit the number of times someone can contribute to the discussion.

During the activity you may intervene to keep the discussion going but avoid calling on particular students. After the discussion ask students who have all their tokens unused and those who have none left (or those who have picked up several and those who have taken none) how they feel about their participation. You may then ask the whole group to think about the desirable distribution of participation, and the possible ways of achieving it. (Adapted from Brandes and Ginnis, 1992.)

Guessing grammar
finding grammatical patterns in sample sentences

Level   elementary/intermediate/advanced
Main goals   peer evaluation and monitoring, generalising from examples
Language focus   passive voice or any other area of grammar
Preparation   handouts for each group with sample sentences

This activity is designed to practise the strategy of inductive discovery of rules, and to leave learners for a while without the authority of the teacher.

Ask students to form groups. If you can, make sure that there is an analytic learner (who is good at discerning fine details and language systems) in each group. Give each group a handout with sample sentences of the grammar you want to teach (see an example in the box below.) Ask them to find similarities and differences in the grammatical patterns or in the use of the same pattern in the sentences. You can make the activity easier by grouping sentences according to the pattern they follow.

At the advanced level, ask students to formulate the rule in writing. Walk around to check solutions and elicit corrections where necessary. Then ask each group to read their rule(s) to the class.

At the elementary or intermediate level, ask students to make up three more sentences using the rule they found. Groups then exchange the new sentences, and decide whether they are correct or not. Allow some time for doubtful issues or ideas that the students may want to ask you or each other about.

Sentence pairs for when to use the passive voice

a I want it to be done today.	I want them to do it today.
b Your shoes need to be cleaned.	Somebody/You should clean your shoes.
c My watch has been stolen.	Someone has stolen my watch.
d His painting was sold for £12,000.	My cousin sold his painting for £12,000.
e She was taken to hospital.	The ambulance took her to hospital.
f Chimney-sweeps are believed to bring good luck.	People believe that chimney-sweeps bring good luck.
g He's been informed about the plot.	Somebody has informed him about the plot.
h The doors must be shut.	You must shut the doors.
i These horrible billboards are put up everywhere in town.	They put up these horrible billboards everywhere in town.
j She was given a bar of chocolate.	Someone gave her a bar of chocolate.

You may use these sentence pairs to get students to determine under what circumstances to use the passive voice. In this case, in *a*, *b*, *d*, *h*, and *i* the passive is used because the action or the object is emphasised instead of the actor in the original sentence. In *c*, *g*, and *j* it is used because the actor is unknown. In *e* and *f*, the actor is obvious.

The dictionary person
using monolingual dictionaries in the classroom

Main goals   self-correction, peer-correction, being the source of information

Language focus   using a monolingual dictionary, spelling
Preparation   a monolingual dictionary appropriate to the level
                        of students

During the lesson students often need to check the spelling, the proper use, or the exact meaning of a word. Sometimes it is best (and usually the fastest) if you answer such questions yourself. However, you may also use such occasions to pass on the role of information providing to the students, and get them to use dictionaries – a skill that they very much need when working on their own. We suggest that you use monolingual dictionaries for this activity because, in our experience, students need more encouragement to use these than bilingual dictionaries.

Bring a dictionary to the lesson, and the first time that a suitable question arises (e.g. what's the correct spelling of *queue*?), ask students if they ever use monolingual dictionaries. Ask one of them (if possible, choose someone who gave a positive answer) to check the word in question (e.g. *queue*) and spell it out aloud. Leave the dictionary with this student for the rest of the lesson, and keep on asking him or her for correction whenever possible. Next time, ask another student to be the 'dictionary person'.

At a later stage, when students are familiar with the task, you can establish a system to ensure that everybody takes on the role of information providing. For example, you may define a route from desk to desk that the dictionary will follow from lesson to lesson.

Variation:
In a small class, after some time you may announce that from now on everybody can use the dictionary any time they need it: just place it somewhere within easy reach and remind students to use it whenever appropriate.

Correcting homework
correcting group mates' homework

Main goal   peer-correction
Language focus   grammar and/or vocabulary review
Preparation   give writing task for homework in previous lesson
Notes   spreads over two or three lessons, but does not
                        necessarily take a long time; may not work out well
                        if students are very sensitive to criticism

When correcting the work of their peers, students are invited to apply the rules of the foreign language consciously and to distance the rules from the authority of the teacher. The activity works best with a homework assignment with a relatively narrow focus on some grammatical pattern or other rule.

Ask students to exchange their solutions to the homework exercise, read each other's work and correct any mistakes they find. If there are students who have not done their homework, either ask them to do it then and there, or ask them to form a pair with someone who has come prepared.

When ready with their corrections, students return the solutions to their author, and then put on a slip of paper any questions they may have about either what they corrected or their own work. Ask students if they have any general questions: they may put these to the class and you can help with eliciting the answers. Then you may collect all their written questions and, as necessary, deal with them individually or in a separate remedy session in the next lesson.

If the main purpose of the homework task was practice, you may not need to look at the students' solutions, since the activity already provided ample feedback for students, and the questions they ask will give you an idea of problem areas.

Variation:

If students are very sensitive to criticism, and especially when it is coming from peers, you may ask them to work in groups, discussing solutions and correcting mistakes together.

Stubborn mistakes
dealing with frequent mistakes in written work

Level	elementary/intermediate/advanced
Main goals	deciding on learning procedures, identifying difficulties
Note	works best as homework
Preparation	photocopies of practice exercises

Some students tend to concentrate only on the mark they receive on their written work and pay little attention to the mistakes you corrected. This activity invites students to learn from their mistakes.

Ask students to read through all the homework they have turned in during the past two to three weeks (or more if they haven't had many written assignments) and make a list of the mistakes that they made more than once. They should group the errors according to type, such as grammar, spelling, or choice of word, and suggest some ways to work on their problems.

In a small class, you may ask students to compare their lists with each other and discuss possible remedies if they have similar problems. In a large class, this may take too long, or create too much confusion, so instead you may read the lists and group students according to their problems for a discussion in the next lesson. For this, you may also prepare a collection of practice exercises for the different groups to choose from. Some students may have very particular problems which you may need to treat individually.

Student-generated test
groups write a test for the class

Level	elementary/intermediate/advanced
Main goals	deciding on learning procedures, producing learning materials, self-evaluation
Language focus	grammar review, written fluency practice
Note	may help you tackle problems with cheating

This activity encourages students to see a test for what it is: a means of measuring their knowledge or identifying problem areas, and something which is useful for them, too, and not only for the teacher. Preparing a test and discussing difficulties arising with peers may require more time than studying for a teacher-written test, but it may considerably increase students' understanding of the material.

You may start by asking students what items of grammar or vocabulary they found most useful or important over the given period, and decide together what should be included in the test. Then assign each set of items to a pair or group of students and ask them to prepare a test. You may provide a set framework (e.g. multiple choice sentences for which they write choices, or a text for a cloze test), a few patterns to choose from, or give them total freedom concerning form.

Depending on the complexity of the material they have to work on, pairs or groups may finish their work during the lesson, or may do the task for homework. Next, collect the completed test pieces, and make any necessary corrections. You may combine the pieces into one comprehensive test which you give to the whole class and then correct and mark them yourself or together with the whole class. If you don't want to use the test results to evaluate individual performance, you can ask groups to work on the test together.

Variation:
Alternatively, you may make each group responsible for the administration of their bit of the test: in this case students get the test items on separate slips of paper (and only the ones written by some other group),

and when they have finished everything, they give their answers to the authors of the test item for correction. This may result in some confusion if there are more than three or four groups, so you may need to help by collecting and redistributing answers and then returning the corrected answers to each student.

Problem sounds
practising difficult sounds

Level	beginner/elementary/intermediate
Main goals	presenting a model of the foreign language, peer-correction, focused listening
Language focus	pronunciation of difficult sounds

Some students are especially skilled in picking up pronunciation contrasts and some of them have learnt to produce sounds consciously. In this activity the role of presenting models and correcting mistakes is passed on to these students and this results in increased individual practice time. Also, it encourages students to listen to and learn from each other, and not to rely solely on the teacher.

When working on a sound that presents a problem for most of the students, show them how to distinguish the particular sound, and how to position their tongue, etc. to produce the sound. It is very useful if you can display minimal pairs or other sample words and a sketch of vocal organs on the blackboard or on the OHP so that students can use the information in the next stage.

Ask the class to produce the sound together, and then ask for volunteers to do it individually. If you find that the volunteers are able to present good models, ask students to get into groups around these students, and spend the next five minutes or so practising the sound with them. Invite 'presenters' to use the information on the blackboard/OHP. Walk around during the activity to see if there are any major problems, but intervene only where it is absolutely essential.

Students present grammar
groups present grammar rules to the class

Level	intermediate/advanced
Main goals	presenting a model of the foreign language, cooperation
Language focus	grammar review, explaining
Preparation	handouts on different areas of grammar

In this activity students teach each other rules of grammar. Besides the benefit of active involvement, presenters can gain a better understanding of the particular rules. Also, being students, they may be better able to pinpoint problem areas than the teacher.

After a progress test or as a follow up to a mistakes analysis exercise (see *Correcting homework* on page 93, or *Stubborn mistakes* on page 94), tell students that you would like them to do a remedy session on the problematic areas of grammar. Together with the students, make up a list of areas you would like to work on, and then ask them to form groups and pick one area each. Ask groups to prepare a coherent, clear presentation and a practice activity for the whole class. As this may take considerable time, you may assign it for homework, supplying the groups with handouts, or ideas on what grammar books or pages in their textbook to use. In subsequent lessons, allow five to ten minutes for each group to teach their area to the others.

Hot-cold-lukewarm
setting objectives

Level	intermediate/advanced
Main goals	deciding on targets, self-evaluation
Language focus	adjectives, future forms
Note	works best midway into the semester

The point of this activity is to have students consciously set objectives in their language learning.

Ask learners to think of themselves from the point of view of the teacher of the foreign language. Ask them to list three strengths (abilities) which they have, and write the opposite of each at the other end of the line. Considering the lines as the continuum between the extreme qualities, ask them to mark where they think they are now. For example, they may write:

good at remembering new words ——— x ———— bad at remembering new words

If they want to, they may share their thoughts with a partner at this point.

Next, ask them to list three language skills they would like to develop and imagine each on a continuum (e.g. think of fluency, reading comprehension, or grammatical accuracy, on a continuum from poor to advanced). Again, they should mark their present position.

For homework, ask them to think about ways in which they could achieve their aims, and write down some suggestions for you. You may then discuss these aims and means with the students individually, or, if possible, in groups where members set similar aims. (Adapted from Brandes and Ginnis, 1992.)

Class contract
agreeing on the rules and objectives of classroom work

Main goals	deciding on rules, deciding on targets, group cohesion
Language focus	arguing and persuading, expressing feelings and preferences
Preparation	list of classroom roles, possible problems, objectives

The class contract is an agreement between you and the students on rules in the classroom, and on the rights and responsibilities of the teacher and the students. Its purpose is to establish a framework for classroom work, that is, to give some guidance on how to behave and to help you and the students to deal with discipline problems. The contract may also include common objectives. In this case it helps create a strong sense of purpose, and provides a basis for the evaluation of progress.

On the one hand, the more influence students have on the framing of the contract, the more likely they are to identify with its contents, and the more likely it is that it will work in practice. On the other hand, the contract only makes sense if you, too, feel comfortable with its contents.

Ideally, you would prepare the contract at the beginning of your work with the students. However, you are most probably reading this book because your students are not yet ready to take responsibility for formulating and keeping such a contract. In this case you need to prepare them first and then introduce the contract at some turning point during your work, such as the beginning of a new semester, so that students feel that they are making a fresh start.

First, write up a list of tasks and roles in the classroom that you think should be settled in the contract, as in the first column of the table on page 99. You may show this to the students and ask them to think about and comment on how these should be handled in the class, and what other issues should be included. Alternatively, you may suggest a possible way to deal with each task or rule (as in the second column) and ask students to change or add to your suggestions as they wish.

Carry on with the discussion until you arrive at a solution acceptable to all. With beginners, this stage should be done in the students' mother tongue; with multilingual beginner or elementary classes you may need to preteach some vocabulary for the activity.

At the end, agree on a form of displaying the contract and on who will prepare the 'official' copy.

For an elaborately presented example of preparing for and working out a class contract, see Puchta and Schratz, 1993.

Example class contract

homework	students who forgot to do their homework must do it for the next lesson and show it to the teacher
absence	is not an acceptable excuse for not having done one's homework
being on time	students and the teacher are ready to start the lesson on time, and owe an apology to each other if they aren't
respecting each other	students listen to each other or the teacher speaking
who talks when	the teacher decides who talks when, except for pair or group work and asking questions or making suggestions
humour	everybody can make humorous remarks as long as they are not disruptive or insulting
working together	each student is willing to cooperate with all other students in the class
the target language	students and the teacher use the target language as much as possible
arranging desks	students do it as quickly and quietly as possible
marking tests	the teacher marks tests within a week (and owes an explanation to the class if failing to do so)

Further reading

Bloor, Meriel and Bloor, Thomas (1988) *Syllabus Negotiation, The Basis of Learner Autonomy*, in Brookes, A. and Grundy, P. (1988) offers a mostly theoretical discussion of an approach to help learners understand and articulate their objectives.

Brandes, Donna and Ginnis, Paul (1992) *A Guide to Student-Centred Learning*, Simon and Schuster Education offers one hundred learner centred activities (not only for language teaching), evaluation and assessment exercises and games, discusses the importance of teacher attitudes, and some ideas of how to deal with resistance from students and/or the school environment.

Brookes, Arthur and Grundy, Peter (eds.) (1988) *Individualisation and Autonomy in Language Learning*, ELT Documents: 131, Modern English Publications and the British Council, is a collection of papers on syllabus negotiation, self-assessment, peer-evaluation, pronunciation improvement and other topics. See especially Riley on the cultural aspects of autonomy development.

Campbell, Colin and Kryszewska, Hanna (1992) *Learner Based Teaching*, 1992, Oxford University Press proposes some ways to involve learners in producing materials for the classroom.

Davis, Paul and Rinvolucri, Mario (1990) *The Confidence Book*, Longman includes a section which describes ways of handing over some of the teacher's authority to the students.

Fried-Booth, Diana L. (1986) *Project Work*, Oxford University Press offers ideas on how to organise project work, and presents some case studies.

Hadfield, Jill (1992) *Classroom Dynamics*, Oxford University Press includes a section on how to involve learners in setting, assessing and resetting goals.

Haines, Simon (1987) *Projects*, Nelson (Longman) offers practical ideas and conveniently photocopiable materials.

Lindsey, Crawford W. (1988) *Teaching Students to Teach Themselves*, Nichols Publ. offers practical ideas (not only in language teaching) on how to transfer tasks and roles to the learner.

Moskowitz, Gertrude (1978) *Caring and Sharing in the Foreign Language Classroom: A Sourcebook on Humanistic Techniques*, Newbury House Publishers is a collection of activities, to build motivation and increase learner involvement.

Puchta, Herbert and Schratz, Michael (1993) *Teaching Teenagers, Model Activity Sequences for Humanistic Language Learning*, Longman describes an example of building up a class contract. Also includes a case study of dealing with a class used to traditional teaching methods.

Ribé, Ramon and Vidal, Núria (1993) *Project Work*, Heinemann offers a step by step guide to setting up a project from creating a good class atmosphere to evaluation, with plenty of practical ideas.

Riley, Philip (1988) *The Ethnography of Autonomy*, in Brookes, Arthur and Grundy, Peter (eds.) (1988) is a mostly theoretical discussion of the possibility of autonomy training running against the culture of students.

Sheerin, Susan (1989) *Self Access*, Oxford University Press offers practical advice on setting up and operating a self access centre.

Tudor, Ian (1996) *Learner Centredness as Language Education*, Cambridge University Press offers a thorough, mostly theoretical discussion of the need for learner centredness, techniques, ideas on peer-correction, error-correction, and how teachers can cope with innovations and changes in their roles.

Wenden, Anita (1991) *Learner Strategies for Learner Autonomy*, Hemel Hempstead, Prentice Hall offers ideas for teachers to prepare themselves for giving over some roles, and also a section on activities.

Willis, Jane (1996) *A Framework for Task-Based Learning*, Longman provides a learner centred technical-theoretical guide to setting up activities that require considerable independence on the students' part.

Appendix

Roles in the classroom

One aim of our book is to help teachers think over the casting of roles in the classroom and perhaps make some changes in their perception and practice. We invite you to consider which classroom tasks you feel the teacher should keep at all times. You may return to the list below a few months later and see if using the activities has changed anything in your classroom practice.

- choosing learning material
- deciding on the procedure for learning
- presenting a model of the target language
- being a source of information and knowledge
- making the final decision in disputes of what is correct or incorrect
- evaluating or giving feedback on student performance
- monitoring/collecting information on student performance
- correcting mistakes
- marking students' work
- rewarding student performance
- keeping discipline in the classroom
- making rules of behaviour in class
- handing out material, collecting papers, etc.
- handling devices used in the classroom
- deciding seating arrangements
- giving instructions to start learners on an activity

For further reading on roles, you may look at chapter 5 in Oxford, 1990, and Wright, 1987.

Sample texts, tests, and role cards

Learning problems
(for *Troubles of the rich and famous* on page 27)

At this time I was considered somewhat backward, but the truth is I did well in those subjects I liked, and failed miserably in those I detested, among which Latin was foremost. However, I managed to survive this hateful subject by a method uncharitable persons might call cheating. And all the while I maintained a simple, steadfast belief that I was destined for higher things . . .
(From Foreman, Carl (1972) *Young Winston: on the life of Winston Churchill,* Fountain Books)

'I preferred the history of naval actions, Don Quixote and Smollett's novels, particularly Roderick Random, and I was passionate for the Roman History. When a boy, I could never bear to read any poetry whatever without disgust and reluctance.'
(From Marchand, Leslie A.(1970) *Byron, a portrait,* Pimlico)

'As I said before, we are all up to X. I could hardly have imagined that a man could be so dull; anyhow I shall not suffer from want of sleep this half . . .'
(J. M. Keynes to Dr. J.N. Keynes, 6th May 1900)
'. . . Rather a provoking boy in school. Reads notes when he should be attending to the lesson. Apt to talk to his neighbour unless severely repressed. He gives one the idea of regarding himself as a privileged boy with perhaps a little intellectual conceit.'
(from the school report on J.M. Keynes, by X, his professor)
(Both excerpts taken from Harrod, Roy (1951) *The life of John Maynard Keynes,* W. W. Norton and Company)

© Cambridge University Press 2000

Simple story
(for *Adding a touch of colour* on page 52 and *Co-authors* on page 67)

A friend invited me to a party. I went there by bus. I got there very late. There were a lot of people at the party. I knew some of them. I met a woman. I danced with her. I asked for her phone number. She is my wife now.

© Cambridge University Press 2000

Cards (for *Facetalking* on page 36)

bored	tired	happy
sad	hurt	surprised
displeased	disappointed	furious
angry	suspicious	frightened
worried	impatient	dreamy
content	relieved	cheerful
sleepy	hot	cold

© Cambridge University Press 2000

Role cards (for *Sharing problems* on page 28)

A	B
Your partner will tell you about his/her problem. Listen very carefully and try to imagine what you would do if you had the same problem. Try to show that you understand the problem, and give some advice if you can.	Think about the problems (real ones) you have in learning English (things like: you forget words, you cannot understand explanations in the lesson, your brother always knows everything better) and tell your partner about these.

© Cambridge University Press 2000

Role cards (for *Close your ears* on page 38)

A	B
You have a problem. Your father got a good job in another city and your parents decided to move there. You like the place where you live, and you have friends in the neighbourhood and in your school. You are afraid of going to a new school. Your parents don't take your worries seriously: they say everything will be OK. But you still feel miserable and don't know what to do. Tell your partner about your problem.	Your partner will tell you about a problem. Look out of the window, clean your nails, yawn if you like, but don't pay any attention. Don't look at your partner while he/she is talking. When he/she has finished, talk about yourself: say something like 'When's the break?', or 'I'm so sleepy', or 'I saw a good film on TV last night.' Do not say anything about your partner's problem.

A	B
You have a problem. Your family decided to go on holiday in the last week of June, the same week when you wanted to go to a camp with your friends. What's more, your parents decided to go to Austria and visit the big museums in Vienna. You hate the smog and the crowds in big cities and you would much rather go to the woods and camp out with your friends, or go to the sea and enjoy water sports. Your parents won't listen to what you want. You are angry and don't know what to do. Tell your partner about your problem.	Your partner is a good friend of yours. He/She looks terribly upset, and you are sure he/she has a problem. Ask what the matter is, and if he/she wants to talk about the problem. While he/she is talking, listen sympathetically. Ask questions. If you are not quite sure about some details, ask about them. Ask how your friend feels and what he/she is going to do. Offer advice. Try to be a good listener.

References

Brandes, Donna and Ginnis, Paul (1992) *A Guide to Student-Centred Learning*, Simon and Schuster Education

Davis, Paul and Rinvolucri, Mario (1990) *The Confidence Book*, Longman

Graham, Caroline (1986) *Small Talk: More Jazz Chants*, Oxford University Press

Haines, Simon (1987) *Projects*, Nelson (Longman)

Kenworthy, Joanne (1987) *Teaching English Pronunciation*, Longman

Oxford, Rebecca (1990) *Language Learning Strategies*, Heinle and Heinle Publishers

Puchta, Herbert and Schratz, Michael (1993) *Teaching Teenagers, Model Activity Sequences for Humanistic Language Learning*, Longman

Ribé, Ramon and Vidal, Núria (1993) *Project Work*, Heinemann

Willing, Ken (1989) *Teaching How to Learn, Learning Strategies in ESL*, National Centre for English Language Teaching and Research, Macquarie University

Wright, Tony (1987) *Roles of Teachers and Learners*, Oxford University Press

Index

Index

Index